PRAISE FOR FLIP-FLOPS AND MICROWAVED FISH

"*Flip-Flops and Microwaved Fish* is a great change of pace when it comes to career advice. Oftentimes, this type of content can be bland, but Yawitz manages to provide a great mix of advice and entertainment that will keep the young professional engaged."

—AJ Vaynerchuk, Co-founder, VaynerMedia, VaynerSports

"Entering organizational life can be dizzying, scary, even terrifying. With wonderful, often sidesplitting humor, Yawitz provides valuable and insightful advice, so navigating the early stages of one's career is far less perilous."

—Michael C. Feiner, former Worldwide Chief People Officer, Pepsi-Cola; award-winning professor, Columbia Business School; author of *The Feiner Points of Leadership*

"*Flip-Flops and Microwaved Fish* candidly introduces you to real life in the workplace, equipping you for success. Full of wish-I-had-knowns and great advice, it will save you from a whole lot of headache and heartache. This is a must-read for any new joiner to the workforce."

—**Leah Cohen-Shohet**, former EVP of Growth & Adoption, Symphony; *Forbes* 30 Under 30 list, 2019

"*Flip-Flops and Microwaved Fish* offers a breezy, commonsensical, and accessible approach to navigating office life for the newly initiated. With a sense of fun, Peter Yawitz of *Someone Else's Dad*, manages to defuse some of the angst surrounding decision-making, while providing sensible direction. I chuckled while reading this and got some good pointers, too!"

—**Regina Resnick**, Sr. Associate Dean and Sr. Managing Director, Columbia Business School Career Management Center

PETER YAWITZ

CREATOR OF *ADVICE FROM SOMEONE ELSE'S DAD*

FLIP-FLOPS

&

MICROWAVED FISH

NAVIGATING

the DOS and DON'TS

of WORKPLACE

CULTURE

GREENLEAF
BOOK GROUP PRESS

Published by Greenleaf Book Group Press
Austin, Texas
www.gbgpress.com

Distributed by Greenleaf Book Group

For ordering information or special discounts for bulk purchases, please contact
Greenleaf Book Group at PO Box 91869, Austin, TX 78709, 512.891.6100.

Design and composition by Greenleaf Book Group and Rachael Brandenburg
Cover design by Greenleaf Book Group and Rachael Brandenburg
Cover image: ©iStockphoto.com/undefined undefined

Publisher's Cataloging-in-Publication data is available.

Print ISBN: 978-1-62634-682-6

eBook ISBN: 978-1-62634-683-3

Part of the Tree Neutral® program, which offsets the number of trees consumed in
the production and printing of this book by taking proactive steps, such as planting
trees in direct proportion to the number of trees used: www.treeneutral.com

Printed in the United States of America on acid-free paper

19 20 21 22 23 24 25   10 9 8 7 6 5 4 3 2 1

First Edition

To my teachers, Daniel and Nora.

CONTENTS

ABOUT ADVICE FROM SOMEONE ELSE'S DAD

Do you run away when your parents offer advice? You're not alone. Most of us want to make our own decisions, and it's natural to resist interference from the people who raised us. We don't want to admit we're nervous or clueless or uncertain. But we can all use some guidance when we're starting out, especially when we feel like outsiders. And face it, just about everyone feels like an outsider at some point.

Advice from Someone Else's Dad (someoneelsesdad.com; @someoneelsesdad) provides great, practical ideas with a humorous edge on how to navigate grown-up-hood. I promise to give you great advice, since I have no skin in your personal game. And if you roll your eyes and grumble after you read my suggestions, I won't even know. Ask your own dad how to handle that one. I'm confident, though, that you'll gain some good insights from me and have a lot of laughs along the way.

As a communication consultant to global companies for about 30 years, I have adapted my advice as technology and generational expectations changed. Slack, videoconferencing, casual attire, open-office plans, and social media have in many cases supplanted the in-office meetings, exhausting travel days, blue suits, closed office doors, and fax machines that were pervasive when I was an eager young office worker who pretended to know everything but often knew very little.

Some things haven't changed. I continue to coach and advise many young workers on diverse topics, such as how to deal with a smelly coworker, how to communicate in an American workplace when you're not American, how to manage a team of peers, how to work with people who take credit for your work, how to make sure emails are clearly written and have the appropriate tone, and how to keep a small talk conversation going without talking merely about the weather. I know also when a question should be directed to a product specialist, lawyer, financial adviser, or cop.

Whether you're worried that you seem like the new kid who's desperately trying to fit in because you look, sound, act, or feel different from the "average" people at work, or you're one of those average people who wants to stand out a bit more, or you consider yourself way above average in everything you do (thanks, Mom and Dad!), I'm sure you'll get some great pointers here on how to get where you want to be.

INTRODUCTION

Day One

It's finally here: your first official day at a new job. Your heart is pounding with nervous excitement, and you can't wait to get to work. You spend your first few hours—or days—filling out paperwork with Human Resources and sitting through mandatory training about what you legally can or can't do or say in the office. During your training you might watch short videos that you're pretty sure were filmed in the 1980s since all the people in them have wide ties, crazy shoulder pads, and big hair. Their collective acting ability stinks.

Eventually you get your ID badge and official photo and learn about systems and processes. So far, so good. Sure, earlier that morning you accidentally opened a door, causing an alarm to screech, and then had to deal with a lengthy interrogation from some burly, humorless guys from Security, but hey, at least no one threw you out in the street (not yet anyway) and said, "Sorry, we made a big mistake hiring you."

Finally, after what seems like an eternity, you get settled at your new workstation, ready to be welcomed by the team you met during your interview process. Some of your new coworkers see you and with big smiles start walking over to greet you. No one, you notice, has big hair.

But suddenly you panic. Where you grew up, men and women who know each other go in for bear hugs. You're almost positive that people aren't supposed to hug and kiss at work, but these excited-looking coworkers are rushing toward you so fast that you're reminded of your family reunions, where crazy Aunt Minnie always bounds over for her annual unwanted slobber. The videos on harassment warned everyone that unwanted affection at work is a big red flag, but you're scared all of a sudden that you'll be forced to deal with a harassment suit within your first five minutes of working here.

Now that you think about it, these coworkers *did* send you some overly friendly emails ("Can't wait to have you join our team!!! Yippee!!☺☺"). Maybe bro hugs *are* the norm here.

Now it seems those coworkers are walking toward you in slow motion—coming in for a very cheery welcome. As they close in, you wonder if they can see the sweat mustache forming over your upper lip or the circles of perspiration appearing under your armpits. Your mind is racing. *Pucker up, bear hug, or handshake? Pucker up, bear hug, or handshake?* You feel your body shaking in anticipation. You're pretty sure you're doing something weird with your lips, and the sweat mustache is starting to drip.

Finally, as your coworkers reach you, they extend their hands. Of course they do; what was that stupid stuff going through your mind? Though your palms are drenched, you gratefully return the gesture. Better a squishy handshake than an inappropriate smooch. That would have been embarrassing. You make a note to yourself: *definitely no kissing, no hugs.* You wish you had known someone to ask for advice about that beforehand.

Later in the day, you're sitting in a colleague's office with the rest of the team, and you notice that one of your coworkers seems to be staring at your feet. You look down also, wondering if you'd stepped in something. But everything looks normal—your shoelaces are tied, your socks aren't slipping down. Maybe your pants are a little short compared to everyone else's. You also observe that in comparison to the dark or fancy striped socks your coworkers are wearing, your white cotton athletic socks really stand out. In fact, they are almost blindingly white. You were told to dress in "business casual," but there was nothing in the welcome manual about appropriate sock type, material, or color. You feel your whole body and persona are screaming to the team, "Outsider!" You try to pull the legs of your trousers a little lower to cover them in case other people start to notice them too, and you wish your mother hadn't sent you a 12-pack of them. Maybe your socks look inappropriate, and maybe, quite possibly, *you* look inappropriate. *Did I dress all wrong for work?* you wonder, feeling uneasy. If only someone had given you advice on this beforehand.

You also notice that your coworkers are using sayings and expressions you're not familiar with. "I'll be out of pocket (*What?*), so don't boil the ocean on this (*Huh?*). But remember, we need to play in the sandbox with them (*Sandbox?*)." Suddenly, you feel like more than just an outsider—you feel as though you've entered an alternate universe. How are you *ever* going to know what people are talking about here?

. . . .

A Note from Dad on Weird Language

Don't panic! Sometimes, even the people using the clichés and expressions don't know what they mean. And some phrases are used more than others in different workplaces. Read on. I'll explain some of the more common sayings later in the book.

. . . .

Your anxiety level is at the near-explosion mark on the stress meter, and you realize that you're much less prepared for working in this office than you thought. You are starting to feel like an imposter and wondering why you were hired.

Whom can you ask about some of this stuff so you're not embarrassed and don't look like you have no idea what's going on? Who can help you figure out what you don't know and communicate effectively in this bizarre new world? Who can reassure you that you *do* belong?

You could ask your dad, you think, but he'll give the same "just-be-a-team-player-and-keep-your-mouth-shut-and-by-the-way-did-you-talk-to-my-college-bud-Ed-about-working-for-him?" speech he's always given you. Thanks, Dad, talk to you soon. Bye.

Advice from Someone Who Knows His Way Around

The best advice you ever received might indeed have been from your own dad, a college professor, a wise but scary-looking old uncle, or maybe even a friend. But not all these people have navigated through different workplace settings. You need to talk to someone who can explain how work *works* in these kinds of situations. (And I'm not talking about your dad's college pal Ed.) Even better, you need to hear from someone who not only is experienced but also has been a longtime consultant to global companies, working with teams and individuals of many nationalities. And since you won't listen to your own dad, or call Ed, you need advice from me, someone else's dad.

People often ask me how to behave, write, and speak when they're dealing with unfamiliar situations such as starting a new job or working with colleagues or clients who come from different cultures. They ask questions like:

- What do my bosses really mean?
- Will people understand my emails?
- What's the polite way to speak up in a meeting?
- Do I really have to answer coworkers who talk to me from adjacent toilet stalls?
- Are white cotton athletic socks *actually* uncool? (Because I *do* have a 12-pack.)
- How can I remain true to who I am and still feel like I belong?

Whether you're someone just starting out in the corporate world, an expat working for an American company, a non-American working for an American company, or a person reentering the workforce after a long time, I'm here to help you, coach you, and answer your questions about how to navigate a new environment or culture when you feel like an outsider. In this book, I share with you my best advice on how to communicate effectively in workplace situations and give you useful tips you can put into practice right away.

Do I have every single answer? No, that would be a much bigger book. But I do offer this as a solid starting point and promise great, actionable advice. And my website, www.someoneelsesdad.com, and social media accounts (@someoneelsesdad) offer advice on even more.

By the way, while I really am someone else's dad, countless people have told me that I've been *like* a dad to them. During the course of my career, young professionals seem to have always gravitated toward me for advice. Maybe, knowing I won't judge them, they find it easier to talk to me than to their own dads. Maybe, by virtue of what I do, I have some additional insights they just haven't heard elsewhere. Maybe, because of the way I am, they like that I make things useful, understandable, and applicable for them. Whatever the reason, I'm glad they think of me that way, and I appreciate being able to step into the role of "Dad" to offer practical, caring, real-world, hopefully entertaining advice on how to manage life at work. I've guided a lot of people in their careers and done it in a way that's made a positive, lasting impact in workplaces.

Even though I've been a communication coach, consultant, teacher, and facilitator for global companies for 30 years, for ten years before that, I was an eager, young employee in fast-paced American workplaces. And I never forgot the anxiety I felt about making basic work decisions and feeling like I didn't fit in. Today I train teams all across the globe, helping them understand cultural differences, personality styles, and expectations to achieve specific goals—anything to ease people's anxieties. I show professionals how and when to communicate, how to manage upward and sideways in a company, and how to deal with personalities, priorities, and peculiarities of their workplace.

I have an undergrad degree from Princeton and an MBA from the Wharton School. I've also taught management communication at Columbia Business School, the MIT Sloan School of Management, and the Tuck School at Dartmouth. And, believe it or not, I've done a lot of comedy writing, lyric writing, and performing about business and communication. (Find me on YouTube and check out "Cliché Bingo," a song I wrote using 85 business buzzwords.) Let me help you find your way in your new workplace. You'll be navigating like a pro in no time. Maybe you'll even be able to show off with some fancy business buzzwords.

I've always been a careful observer of how people interact (or don't interact) at work. I've seen how seemingly innocuous words, comments, behaviors, and even body language affect people both positively and negatively. And I've watched bright young people from different regions and cultures struggle to understand and navigate different work environments, customs, personality types, hierarchies, and ways of communicating. Maybe it's the dad in me, but it's hard for me to see young professionals having a hard time when I know I could help them do something about it. So here it is, a book that offers you the practical advice and useful tips you need for dealing with life and people in different workplaces.

And don't ever worry that you should be like everyone else. Companies thrive when their workforce is made up of people with diverse backgrounds, experiences, and ways of thinking. Just because everyone else goes to the trendy salad place and buys $20 super greens for lunch doesn't mean that you can't bring in a container of leftover stew. Don't change who you are, just be aware of cultural norms. You *do* belong.

Think of this as a reference guide of sorts. You can read through it from start to finish or skip around to find answers to questions you have. You don't need to tackle each topic I cover in this book, but at some point in your career if you find yourself looking for advice, flip through the pages in the section that applies.

Here's my first bit of dad advice: Put on sunscreen even when it's cloudy out, make sure you drink plenty of water, always use good grammar, and call me once a week so I at least know you're alive. I'm kidding; you decide how much water you need. My advice will be better than that. But don't forget the sunscreen.

One

A NEW WORKPLACE

I don't want to generalize about a "typical" person or workplace. That would probably not help you a whole lot since there's tremendous diversity of experience with different companies and, for that matter, with different personality types. A successful company can be located in an old, unrenovated industrial space, where your multinational office mates go to work every day wearing ratty clothes and put their feet up on broken-down, rickety furniture. A successful company can just as easily operate in a sleek, ultra-finished urban office, where the only sound might seem to come from the stylish, ultra-polished shoes of busy, ultra-polished employees on expensive, ultra-plush carpets. Your coworkers might be ambitious or relaxed, bold or reserved, risk-taking or cautious, and everything in between.

For the purposes of familiarizing you with some of the terrain, I think we might be able to at least make *some* generalities about what many business leaders and companies strive to achieve. And the most general goal is to be successful.

Success, however, can mean different things to different leaders. And how those leaders aim to reach their goals can have a strong effect on the work environment. For example, one leader's fiercely competitive way of achieving success can pervade a corporate culture. If all employees buy into that way of working, success may be easier to attain.

A problem can arise when merging companies with very different cultures have a hard time getting Company A's employees to do things the way Company B has always done them. How does everyone achieve success together now?

What to Know about People at Work

Most people are reasonably friendly and receptive at work. Sure, grumpy, shy, inflexible, rude, nasty, and overall weird people find their ways into offices. Still, the openness many Americans display can perplex people who come from parts of the world where employees are expected to conform to more prescribed roles or more traditional social behaviors. It's not uncommon for managers in the US to ask about employees' spouses and kids, their hobbies and interests, and details about how they spent their weekends, because they have a genuine interest in knowing about others' lives outside of work. As long as the questions stay within reasonable professional bounds—meaning staying away from topics you don't consider too personal or uncomfortable—you'll likely find yourself chatting from time to time about things you do outside of work.

To help you start out right, keep in mind three types of people with common but challenging communication styles you may encounter at work: 1) people who are direct; 2) people who are passive; and 3) people who are passive-aggressive.

People Who Are Direct

In general, businesspeople try to accomplish a lot in a day, so they tend to like to get information quickly. People with a direct, fast-paced style may speak quickly, brashly, or candidly. They might send prompt replies to emails, approach you at your desk, and want tasks to be completed sooner than you might expect. It's not uncommon for impatient businesspeople to twirl their index fingers in a circle to signify "speed it up" if a story or message they're listening to is dragging on too long. If you're not familiar with these cues, you might not recognize someone else's impatience. (By the way, some say this behavior is "aggressive." I dislike that label because the underlying meaning connotes force and potential nastiness. And while there are people around who fit that description, I want to focus on the much more "direct" style in which people want everyone to get the point of something as quickly as possible.)

Coworkers who have a direct way of communicating may say things like:

- "Don't beat around the bush."
- "So what's the bottom line?"
- "Let's cut to the chase."
- "Net net."
- "At the end of the day . . ."
- "Get to the point."
- "Just give me the headline."

All these expressions mean the same thing: "Quickly tell me what your main point, conclusion, or request is." And the subtext is, "Stop wasting my limited time with unnecessary details."

Many people unfamiliar with direct communicators have come to me in a panic. My primary advice is not to take impatience personally. In most cases, people who are being direct don't mean to be rude. If you learn how to take their directness at face value and respond appropriately, your interaction with them will be more effective, and you'll do better at work.

To best communicate with coworkers and supervisors who have direct styles, practice getting to the point more quickly. Your cultural background or brain's unique wiring may require you to work harder. Our minds work in a linear way: point 1, point 2, point 3; therefore, conclusion. Training yourself to bypass the points to get quickly to the conclusion takes practice. We'll discuss how to do this more in chapter 5, "The Right Way to Write."

Many non-Americans I've worked with have a very difficult time answering quick questions about what they're trying to tell or sell at work because their schooling emphasized presenting lots of background before getting to a conclusion. "Before I tell you what I need, let me go back to the history of the world and how we got there. Back in the Middle Ages . . ."

In French schools, for example, students are taught from a very young age how to create an argument by formulating a thesis (*la thèse*), presenting a contrarian view with an antithesis (*l'antithèse*), and concluding with a synthesis (*la synthèse*). Since they learned this method early in life, many French businesspeople have had to adjust their thought process to present *la synthèse* up front, which requires them to be intentional in their approach and thinking. But they do it because that's how you interact successfully with people who have a direct communication style.

A Chinese client once told me she totally bombed at a presentation at a US financial firm because culturally she wasn't prepared with the kind of communication skills that would help her persuade a group of fast-paced US bankers. She said in China people would be considered rude if they tried to make a direct recommendation at the outset of a meeting. To illustrate this client's cultural context, she told me to imagine a drawing of a large spiral with a big dot in the middle and a loose end on the outside. In China the actual recommendation would be at the dot in the center, but you would never go there first, and maybe you would never even get there at all. Instead, she said, you would start speaking obliquely, as though you were beginning at the loose end, then make your way inward, getting more and more specific as you slowly moved toward the center. Once it becomes apparent where you're going with your message, decision makers may start to nod slowly, then eventually more rapidly to demonstrate that they "get it." And once you realize that the decision maker understands your recommendation (I guess all that nodding would be the big clue), you would stop talking, even though you might not have arrived at that dot in the center. In Chinese cultural context, this would help lead to a mutual understanding or successful outcome. But in a cultural context in which some leaders and peers gravitate toward a direct style of communication, this would potentially lead to frustration, miscommunication, misalignment of goals, or an unrealized outcome.

Don't let others' direct styles upset you or make you think you're incompetent because your mind doesn't work as fast as theirs. When you work with very direct people, you may have to prepare a bit more before you speak or write to them. For example, think about presenting at the outset the main conclusions from a study you prepared and then present the supporting points. Remember that being direct doesn't mean being abrupt; being direct and polite at the same time will be the way to go.

People Who Are Passive

On the other end of the spectrum are people who apologize for things they do or who won't or can't commit to a position. I don't want to get into these people's psychological profiles, but working with them can be as challenging as working with the direct types.

For example, because they have a hard time making decisions, passive people may ask you to research many options, listen to what you've come up with, and then ask what you think they should do. Since the original task was simply to research, you may not be prepared to come up with recommendations, especially if you don't know all the relevant factors that would go into a suitable decision.

Similarly, passive managers may not be clear about a team's goals because they fear they'll make the wrong decision. In these situations, team members typically become frustrated because they haven't been given any directions about how to prioritize tasks.

While this list isn't comprehensive, I've put together some things you might hear passive people say. Note that many are apologetic and show a lack of confidence:

- "I hope you don't mind me giving my opinion . . ."
- "I'm probably way off base here, and I bet I'm wrong, and this comment surely won't add anything to our conversation, but . . ."
- "Hmm, um, I'm not sure what makes the most sense."
- "I agree, but then again, the alternatives do have lots of merits."
- "I sort of agree."
- "I haven't the slightest idea how to approach that."
- "Maybe if you look at everything, the solution will magically appear."

If you do work with or for passive people, you may have to find opportunities to encourage them and validate their opinions. Here are examples of things you might try:

- You might need to say things like, "I think your idea makes a lot of sense, and here's why."
- You may have to ask how to prioritize your tasks, all the while challenging and pushing for definite action steps, by saying something like, "I agree that these are the right things to work on right now, but can we discuss which items are the most urgent so I know when you'd like each done?" If you don't get much of an answer, you may have to say, "Well, let's discuss each item and figure out a timeline."
- You may have to ask about the rationale behind certain tasks so you'll be better prepared to help come up with a decision. Even something direct, such as saying, "I'd be happy to look at the options. I'll put in my preliminary recommendations based on what I find," is good.

People Who Are Passive-Aggressive

There are others who avoid conflict or confrontation and have their own way of communicating, which can baffle those who need more precise information or validation. A coworker with a passive-aggressive style might say something like, "If someone had given me the percentage change in revenue this year, I would have been happy." The underlying meaning to their statement could actually have been:

· "You should have included that percentage."

· "I should have given you more instructions."

· "You did a nice job, but I'm being picky."

· "I love playing mind games."

Another person with a passive-aggressive style might nod and stare at you rather than say anything. Imagine going to a meeting attended by a bunch of passive-aggressive people. You could easily sit there thinking that you're in the middle of some bizarro workplace. You might hear undercurrents of messages, notice discreet eye rolls and stares, and feel uncomfortable with the overall vibe.

The problem for everyone is that if messages aren't communicated explicitly, people could easily walk away from the meeting having very little idea about what anyone was thinking, making it difficult to follow through with a plan of action. When no one knows where things stand, no one can fully perform job functions or gauge effectiveness at work.

So what's the best way to work alongside coworkers with passive-aggressive communication styles? My advice is to always ask politely for clarification if messages are even slightly ambiguous. Your passive-aggressive coworkers might not like this request, but you need to be able to do your job.

Below is a table showing a few statements passive-aggressive people sometimes make. It includes examples of possible interpretations of each of the statements, a suggestion for what they should have said to be clearer, and potential reasons why they said what they said.

Whenever possible, try not to leave a conversation with passive-aggressive people without clarifying what they really mean.

When they say . . .	"Get it done whenever you get a chance."	"Nice job."	"I hate this."
They could mean . . .	"I really need it within the hour."	"I haven't looked at it."	"I hate this."
But they could also mean . . .	"I'm giving you nonsense busy-work since I can't think of anything else for you to do."	"It's not great, but at least you got it done."	"I really hate this."
But they really should have said . . .	"I'd like you to finish this task within the hour because I'd like to proofread it before I email it to my boss later today."	"Here's what I think is great, and here's what I'd like you to revise."	"Let me tell you why this isn't what we want."
And they didn't say that because . . .	They worry that you will think they're too demanding and pushy if they are too direct.	It's hard to spend time giving feedback.	They don't realize that being overly direct can upset people.

Of course, the direct, passive, and passive-aggressive styles are not by any means the only styles you'll see at work. Also, there's no need to figure out where *you* are on a spectrum of passive/direct/passive-aggressive behaviors. Your job is to be assertive, polite, and authentic. And your job will always be to make sure you know what your managers want and give them what they want (otherwise why would they pay you?).

Is One Jerk a Company Bellwether?

Dear Someone Else's Dad,

I'm in business school, and one day a guest from a financial services firm made a presentation but then kept interrupting students who asked him questions. He kept saying things like "Out with it! What's your question?" I was interested to learn more, but he wound up offending me so much that I didn't bother asking anything. Should I assume that's how things work at his company? (Because if so, I'm not sure I'd ever want a job there!)

Thanks,

Offended Recruit

Dear OR,

What a moron! If this guy's behavior represents the norm at his company, I don't blame you for feeling like you don't want to work there. Companies normally take very seriously how their employees represent them, and I bet his company's leadership team would have been pretty upset to learn that this person was its poster child that day. In fact, you should let the recruiter know what you experienced; the feedback will quickly get back to the company.

Though direct people can be scary and off-putting, don't completely write off the company based on one jerk. Find ways to meet other people at the company and see how they treat you, as well as each other. If everyone you meet barks at one another, then your initial instinct was right. The place may not be a fit for you, but it might be a great place for those who thrive on high intensity/high stakes/high energy/high rudeness.

What to Know about Workplaces

Many young people get their first taste of what an American office is like from watching videos of the NBC sitcom *The Office*. The show is indeed very funny with its mix of inept, ultra-serious, and awkward characters placed in situations that are sometimes outlandish. Unfortunately, some American workplaces (and British ones, considering that *The Office* was first a UK show starring Ricky Gervais) aren't that far off the mark of *The Office* (though I hope, for your sake, you don't have to work there). I've certainly met my share of Michaels (like the callous egotistical boss played by Steve Carell) and Dwights (like the officious but naïve salesman played by Rainn Wilson) along the way. While the real versions of these personality types may not be as extreme as the ones you see on TV, coworkers' quirks do have the ability to get on your nerves, especially since you spend a good portion of your waking hours with your supervisors, peers, and support staff.

And that's what you'll be doing: spending a *lot* of time with people whom you might not otherwise choose as your family or friends. Remember that guy who lived down the hall in your college dorm who would stop by and never leave, even if you gave the most obvious hints, like not making eye contact, not laughing or responding to anything he said, and even turning off the lights and leaving him in the room in the dark? Or that know-it-all woman in your class who monopolized every conversation and pretended she and the professor were long-lost twins ("Oh my God, we are so alike!")? What about the person you were partnered with for a big assignment who didn't do any of the work but then, on the day of your big presentation, acted like the person in charge and took all the credit for the work ("I spent hours researching this and made some amazing discoveries.")?

Anytime you work with someone else, you have the potential to deal with those who think and act differently from you and have different backgrounds and experiences; it's the sum of all these personalities that contributes to a workplace culture.

You have a role to play in building up a positive and successful workplace culture too. Regardless of whether you're familiar with local cultural norms or not, you have a voice, particular skills and talents, and a history and background that adds to a company. Hopefully, you'll find your way into a workplace that recognizes and is enriched by your unique contribution. And often it's the different worldviews we bring that actually make a place better.

In addition to people, there are other factors that inform a workplace culture. For the most part, many companies try to do what they can to make going to work a pleasant experience. For example, the open-office plan, in which there are no walls and coworkers sit together, is a strategy that encourages collaboration. The cubicle culture, in which people are separated from one another by moderately soundproof half-walls, is also common, giving coworkers a combination of privacy, relative anonymity, and annoyance if their neighbor is loud.

Whichever way an office is set up, companies often also create spaces where employees can gather to brainstorm or engage in small talk—a small conference room, a comfy couch by a window, a kitchen, a game room, or a snack area. Companies generally want you to be able to engage in dialogue, connect with your coworkers, and have your voice heard. They believe these things lead to your satisfaction as an employee, partly because when people are happy and morale is high, there's more productivity, a better chance for good ideas, and improved opportunity for company success.

Workplace Culture

During the orientation for a new job, you might learn about how your company defines its mission and its culture. The *mission* describes what the company does and why. The *culture* is about how people work together and what the company values. Together, mission, culture, and value statements should provide insight into how employees should behave, work together, and measure success.

To best demonstrate how a mission statement works, let's start with a simple example. Let's say I decide to open a lemonade stand on a sidewalk adjacent to a busy corner in a neighborhood in Supertown. My mission statement for my new business might be:

> I sell lemonade so thirsty people can get a drink.

That statement is absolutely fine for my first day in business. After all, that's what I do. But if I want to motivate my employees and move to the next level of success (defined perhaps by the number of cups I sell each day), I may have to rejigger my message to something more like this:

> We sell the best lemonade with the utmost friendliness and professionalism to everyone in Supertown.

That's much better. But let's suppose a competitor opens a lemonade stand on the other side of the intersection from where I'm located. I might have to change my business plan a bit and also redefine my mission in order to ensure that I do good business:

> We provide freshly squeezed lemonade and a variety of the highest-quality, organic, locally baked goods with a smile to everyone in the community.

I added some necessary focus and dimension to my business and made sure this was reflected in my new mission statement. The statement for my company—or for any company—should clearly define what it does and why. The mission statement provides a reference point to remind everyone why they are doing what they are doing. In my lemonade stand example, I would expect all my employees to be proud of and tout our "highest quality" goods and truly be eager to smile at everyone in the community no matter how much that may hurt the inside of their cheeks.

The fact that I needed to figure out the best way to define myself as a business isn't unique. Corporations spend a lot of time refining their mission statements in the pursuit of excellence. Mission statements are often created by committee, and words are agonized over to make sure everyone feels that the message is correct.

Many business magazines, books, and websites feature lists of the best places to live, the best CEOs, the best industry analysts, the best design firms, the best websites, the best and most upcoming entrepreneurs, etc. Some companies even have specific people on staff to make sure that the company and its talent are represented on the appropriate best-of lists.

The important thing for you is to get to know and understand your company's mission statement and try to see how your job fits in with the overall strategy. Also, pay attention to the decisions the senior leaders of your company make. New initiatives typically follow the mission. When they don't—perhaps because of industry disruptions or other competitive or financial threats, or even bad management—the mission may be tweaked again. Be aware of any changes and take your cues from management about how a tweaked mission statement will specifically affect your group.

Culture Fit

You may see something called a culture statement, a values statement, or a set of company values framed on the wall or embossed on coffee mugs, notepads, or toilet paper. OK, I never looked *that* closely. (If you hunt around a storage closet, you may find some mouse pads that no one uses anymore. They make pretty good potholders.)

Ultimately, companies' value statements are designed to remind employees how to behave and, in turn, show clients and investors how a company does business and how its employees behave.

Defined corporate culture and values are actually quite important, and the more employees and teams stray from what the core values are, the more trouble can arise. For instance, I once worked with a company whose corporate culture revolved around open communication (now commonly called transparency), shared common goals, and strong collaboration with respect for hierarchy. Members of one team at this company withheld information from one another and communicated solely by email, even though they sat next to each other and could easily have swiveled their desk chairs around to chat.

We had to remind everyone of the well-defined value statement as a way for them to recognize that the way they were working was not only inefficient but also went against everything the company stood for. As a first step, we scheduled regular and well-planned "huddles" (sometimes just swiveling their chairs so everyone faced one another) so the entire team could be updated on issues. We then banned the use of email to ask a question if an in-person chat could do. This new process built better camaraderie and offered the team the opportunity to recruit other people to collaborate on projects together. This example is a reminder that a company's stated values should provide a good blueprint of how all coworkers, from top to bottom, should behave.

I highly recommend that you get to know a company's stated values before you start working there. Knowing what a company stands for will help you get a sense of whether your personal values match. You'll also find that you'll have a better sense of purpose from day one.

If you don't know your company's value and mission statements, you may be able to find them on the company's website. Large, publicly traded companies will often include this information somewhere in an investor relations section. Otherwise, you should ask and look around by checking out websites like glassdoor.com to find insights from former employees and by talking with people you know who work there. Just be aware that some posters on company review websites might be disgruntled employees or ex-employees, so take some reviews with a grain of salt.

I once turned down a consulting job because I knew I wouldn't enjoy the culture, which was described to me as hypercompetitive. The company told me that its employees liked to play intense games during training sessions because winning was everything. That was important for me to hear. While a winning-is-everything culture might work great for the company (which does very well) and for the people who thrive in that environment, I knew myself well enough to recognize that I would probably do OK in but not genuinely like that kind of culture. You might be the kind of person who would really enjoy working in that culture, in which case, reading the company's values statement would have helped you affirm your decision to join the company. My point is that it's well worth your time to research a company to try to determine if its culture is a good fit for you. If it's not, you might only last so long.

Forget What We Told You Yesterday

Dear Someone Else's Dad,
The values statement of my company changes monthly. Is that normal?
Thanks,
Valued Employee

Dear VE,
While mission statements may change from time to time as business climates are disrupted or divisions are sold off, values statements should remain static. Sometimes companies tweak their values statements slightly to make sure that they are fostering more inclusiveness. Other times a culture may change if a company is acquired and has new leadership. But I'd be a bit suspicious about why your company keeps changing its values, just as I would be if a friend changed his values every month. If the new values statement is at odds with the previous one(s), which would be even more odd, ask your manager how the updated statement is supposed to translate into how you behave toward others and toward your job at hand.

Cultural Cues

Sometimes a corporate culture statement for a global company can be at odds with the local culture of a foreign branch office or of those with whom it does business. A statement like "We foster a culture of intense intellectual debate, which allows us to devise the best solutions, achieve superior financial returns, and reduce risk" can seem a bit scary in a regional office where the local culture is more often characterized as cooperative and collaborative and where disagreement can come across as disrespectful or rude.

So what happens when two cultures are at odds with one another, and you work for a company that champions doing things in a specific way? If, for example, you were an employee in a regional office, you might have to learn to play two roles: being more competitive when dealing with the home office, but showing a different and more collaborative side when dealing with local clients and vendors.

On the other hand, if the main corporate culture is one in which everyone is expected to get to the point in both written and spoken work, that culture will have to win, no matter where you work or what context you're in. This is difficult to do. In fact, I've had to help many professionals change the way they think about and approach their methods of communication, helping them learn to adjust to more up-front and to-the-point styles.

Another cultural problem occurs when native English speakers use phrases that don't translate well. For example, let's say someone in an American office emails a sentence like "This system is totally out of control" to describe a rather simple problem. A person reading the email in a different country might literally assume that disaster has struck, whereas the writer might simply have meant that the system is not working as expected. There's no quick solution to the problem of understanding idioms except I'd recommend that people avoid using them when non-native speakers are part of a conversation, and that people who hear something that makes no logical sense ("He went totally postal!"[1]) ask for some clarification.

---

1   "Going postal" refers to a rash of gun rampages at US post offices in the late 1980s by mentally unstable postal workers. The ridiculous idiom is used to mean that someone is about to go on some sort of rampage.

In addition, local nonverbal cues and customs, which we'll cover in chapter 3, "The Unspoken Stuff," can cause big misinterpretations. Think of how many times you do any of the following in a day: roll your eyes, smirk, sigh, do a head-turn, fold your arms. Those small movements, things you may not realize you're doing, can speak volumes to someone from a different culture. Sending the wrong message to coworkers, clients, or those outside your company, even through simple words and phrases or nonverbal cues, can significantly affect the way you're able to work and interact with others.

It would be impossible to learn every single cultural cue you might encounter. Some of that you'll discover as you go along by simply observing those around you. But I do think it's important to not only understand how to give and take cultural cues from your coworkers but also to develop an awareness of what some of those cues are. If you have the skills to recognize different kinds of cultural communication, you'll be able to work with others more effectively and figure out how to fit in with your company, even if you have coworkers named Michael and Dwight.

Not Sure I Fit In

Dear Someone Else's Dad,

I work for a very successful American start-up, which has a flat, nonhierarchical culture, and people are encouraged to be open and creative. I knew this when I applied for my job, and I forced myself to show enthusiasm for this type of workplace during my interview, even though I was brought up in an Asian culture where people are encouraged to be reserved and respect authority. I really like what I do, and the perks and people are great, but I constantly feel pressure to pitch new ideas in meetings, approach "managers" anytime, and demonstrate what an amazing opportunity it

is to be here—all things that don't come naturally to me. Do you think I'd be happier at a more traditional organization?
Thanks,
Square Peg

Dear SP,

I think everyone working in a new environment can relate to feeling like a square peg being pushed into a round hole and desperately trying to smooth out personal edges just to fit in. I'm going to focus on two comments you made: 1) that you like the work, people, and perks, and 2) that the company appreciates openness and creativity. On the first point, don't discount how important job satisfaction is in terms of your career development and personal well-being. I know you feel pressure about coming up with ideas all the time, but you have to ask yourself what's worth more—potentially investing in ways to improve your communication skills and growing along with your current company, or finding a less satisfying position where you just do as you're told.

Which brings me to my second point: if your "managers" are open to new ideas and ways of operating and thinking, they should also be open to how people work. You might tell them that you love your job but feel a lot of pressure to come up with ideas and need to find other ways to support the team. Not all ideas have to be million-dollar ones. Sometimes even small suggestions on workplace efficiency can add value.

What to Know about the Workday

Way back in 1980, the title of the movie *9 to 5* was immediately recognizable to anyone who had ever worked in an office. Offices would typically start business at 9 AM and almost completely clear out at a real or virtual 5 PM bell. When someone asked for something to be completed by close of business, or "COB," the implicit time was exactly 5 PM. Some offices still operate on an in-office 9–5 schedule, but nowadays hours are all over the place, and people work from all over the place.

Another cultural shift is the blurring between being at work and not at work. More people are working remotely, and we're seeing that the way to succeed in a company may not be affected by whether we're physically there or not. Many businesspeople, even those who don't work for large companies, are often online long after an eight-hour workday; some make themselves available 24/7. If someone tells you to complete something by COB these days, you better clarify what time that's really supposed to be.

The French Disconnection

Did you know that there's a French law allowing workers the right to disconnect and to ignore emails outside of working hours? The next time you receive a demanding email from your American boss over the weekend, I dare you to email back: *"Excusez-moi, mais une loi française m'empêche de répondre à votre courriel jusqu'à mon retour au travail lundi matin. Merci."* (Thanks, five years of high school French and Google Translate, which helped me with "Excuse me, but a French law prevents me from responding to your email until I get back to work on Monday morning. Thank you.")

Hours in the office in different locations and industries are variable. Some industries and offices expect employees to dutifully work on a set schedule. It's not unusual for West Coast financial firms to expect employees to keep Eastern time zone hours to follow the stock market's open and close. In Silicon Valley, technology firms often pride themselves on helping commuting employees by providing Wi-Fi-enabled shuttle buses, partly because they want their employees to be online and available most of the time.

Workers in very competitive industries—think consulting, banking, and high tech—may even brag about how long they worked in a day. "Oh, man," a coworker might say, "I was at my desk until two in the morning and back again at seven."

"Two?" another coworker might reply. "I was at my desk the entire night and didn't even have dinner."

"No dinner?" a third coworker might say. "I was at the LA office till nine, rushed to the airport to catch a red-eye, worked on the plane all night, and by the time I came straight to the office, I realized the only thing I'd eaten in 48 hours was one small bag of stale airline peanuts."

That's when the fourth coworker, who'd just run a marathon, might say, "A whole bag of peanuts? I slept under my desk every night for nine days, eating only the crumbs that my old officemate dropped on the carpet before he quit his job a couple of months ago."

Follow all this with a chorus of "Wow!" "Amazing!" "Great job!" "You're going places, buddy!"

Realistic? Maybe. But there are many companies in which the number of hours people work is considered an accomplishment they would proudly boast about on Twitter. I've seen posts that say things like "Sleep? Whoops, forgot to put it on the schedule!" I don't know why I'm supposed to be impressed by that one. I'll talk more about managing life, work, and expectations in later chapters, but I do want to set some expectations here in the early part of the book.

Think about the kind of company you're going to work for and consider what you're willing to put in. If you're just starting out in your career or preparing to advance to a higher role, you might be inclined to do a longer workday. Or you might want to do your research and find a company that has a culture and workday more suited to your style and priorities.

I applaud whatever work schedule you choose to arrange for yourself. But see if you can find out the company norms about face time in the office versus quiet time working from home or a coffee shop. I don't recommend showing what a martyr you are by spending an entire night in the office working on a particular task. (On the flip side, some people might question why you needed to spend all night doing work that someone else might have completed in a few hours.)

I'm not suggesting you should shy away from long hours and hard work. Everyone should enjoy something they're doing so much that they get fully absorbed in it. Here's one of the best pieces of advice I can give you: do your work, do it well, and don't brag about it.

. . . .

Promising the Impossible

A client once told me that her boss said, "We're not just available 24/7; we're available 36/8!" I was floored because the comment makes no sense a) in English or b) in nature. This ridiculous statement shows how much people will boast about things that are impossible to do just to prove how great they are. I wonder if anyone ever challenged (or fired) that boss.

. . . .

What's Wrong with Eating Out?

Dear Someone Else's Dad,

I'm Brazilian and just started work in LA. In São Paulo, it's typical to take an hour-and-a-half break for lunch at a local restaurant (partially government-subsidized). In my LA office, people grab something and eat fast at their desks. Does anyone ever go out, and am I expected to eat lunch at my desk every day?

Thanks,

Paulista

Dear Paulista,

Yes, people do go out for lunch sometimes; it can be a great time for people on a team to get to know one another better. But at some American offices, it's not an everyday occurrence. Since Americans' lunches aren't subsidized by the government and only sometimes covered by a company, many people try to keep their personal expenses down and take advantage of either takeaway options or bring their lunch from home. Don't be pressured into working through lunch at your desk every day. Taking a break from work isn't a bad thing. Enjoy the California sunshine, and don't forget the sunscreen.

Two

EVERYTHING COMMUNICATES

A lot of things you wonder about might seem like minor basics when you start a new job: whether to shake hands or not when greeting someone; whether to dress like everyone else or in your own style; whether to pretend to know what people are talking about or just go hide behind a tall office plant. While none of these issues is a matter of life or death, I think you should be aware that they're not actually as minor as you may believe. In business, everything you do, wear, say, write, or hide behind communicates something. How you present yourself to people affects the way they perceive and interact with you. And particularly when you're new, first impressions can be hard to change.

I once ran a seminar for young professionals in which I gave an example of a person who did everything wrong in a professional context: regularly interrupting others, putting his feet on a chair, laughing at people's suggestions, chewing gum loudly, and texting during meetings. I asked the group how they thought the guy in my example could improve in order not to jeopardize his career. One eager participant answered, "He's got to show that he's some baller," which communicated two key things to me:

- She assumed I knew what the term "baller" meant. (I didn't.)
- I realized I wasn't at all up-to-date on cool, new expressions. (I hope the word *cool* is still used.)

I later learned that a baller simply refers to someone who plays ball well. (In my day, we'd call this kind of person a rock star.) Although I had no idea what the eager seminar participant was talking about at first, she was right—in order to do well at that company, the employee I described would have to show that he is a major baller, a great hire, an amazing worker, and as far as I'm concerned, a rock star. He would need to not only correct those behaviors by demonstrating great professionalism and responsibility but also by working hard to change the perception others have of him. And that's easier said than done.

At the beginning of communication-training seminars I conduct, I almost always ask the participants what qualities they believe make an effective communicator. Pretty much everyone brings up the same things: being clear, being concise, being engaging, demonstrating expertise, speaking clearly, relating the topic to the audience, etc. The participants are absolutely right; those are indeed qualities people should master in order to communicate well.

But I also point out that we all very quickly make judgments about people based on certain behaviors, actions, or qualities we see in them. The judgments we make can color our impressions and, when they are negative, make it hard for us to see people as valuable assets to the organization.

Here's an example: Let's say Paulo, a new member of the team whom few people have met, walks into a scheduled meeting five minutes late. Here are some impressions people in the room may have of him as he joins the meeting:

- He's undependable and irresponsible.
- He's showing that other things are more important than the meeting.
- He's never had to do anything responsible in his life. (Hey, some people may be thinking something extreme like this.)

· He does not care enough about this job.

· He needs to be more organized.

· He is going to be late every time.

Maybe Paulo had a legitimate excuse for being late. He could have been on the phone with a client or his manager and was unable to end the call before the meeting started. Perhaps the person who had led his orientation session forgot to show Paulo how to find his way around this particular floor. Maybe Paulo's subway train had had a sudden power outage, and he'd been stuck across town without cell service.

Or maybe Paulo didn't have a legitimate reason for being late. Perhaps where he comes from, it is considered the norm to show up five minutes late. Perhaps people's other perceptions of him are true.

Regardless, his act of walking into the meeting late communicated something to the people who were there. If their initial impression of him is uniformly negative, it could take a while for Paulo to counteract that impression and to demonstrate to his new coworkers that he is a baller . . . sorry, a rock star . . . sorry, a responsible team member.

What does this mean for you? Like it or not, everything you do or don't do at work communicates something about you: how you dress, when you show up, what foods you eat, what phrases you use, how much you smile, what photo you use as your desktop wallpaper, and in some cases, even whether you keep your office door open or closed all day.

In this chapter, I'll cover the basics of what communicates well in the workplace, how you can fit in at a new company, and how you can shape the perception people have of you so you have a positive, productive experience in your job. Whether it's the right kind of etiquette for greeting others, the appropriate outfit to wear, or strategies for remembering people's names, you'll find the practical information you'll need to communicate the right things about yourself at work. It's important to be honest and true to who you are but also have an awareness that everything communicates.

· ·

Behaviors That May Have Unintended Consequences

Here are some things you may do that can make people judge you, fairly or unfairly:

- Showing up late to a meeting
- Checking your phone during a meeting
- Surfing the web, emailing, buying things on Amazon, checking sports scores, or anything else you do on your laptop aside from taking notes about the meeting
- Forgetting to bring something to write with
- Eating, unless it's a breakfast or lunch meeting
- Speaking with your mouth full during a breakfast or lunch meeting
- Using offensive humor or language
- Speaking inappropriately or harshly about others
- Laughing uncontrollably about a trivial matter
- Putting on a face mask and napping
- Napping without a face mask
- Wearing earbuds
- Mumbling, speaking too softly, or shouting
- Engaging in side conversations in a language others in the room don't understand
- Over-nodding and over-smiling
- Clipping your fingernails (or toenails)
- Looking bored
- Sighing
- Rolling your eyes
- Standing up and suddenly singing an aria from *La Traviata*
- Swigging from a flask

· ·

Here are a few beginner "protips" to help set your thinking. There's no situation that exactly matches another, but you can take some steps to set yourself up for success at work.

Find out what the regional and corporate norms are. Watch others in meetings to see where people sit, which people participate, how people offer opinions, and how people present themselves. Don't ever be afraid to ask a peer before a meeting what behaviors and actions are typically expected in the workplace. Most of your coworkers will gladly give you advice about company-specific dos and don'ts, such as whether you can eat during meetings or whether your phone should be out of sight. If there's not a clear consensus about whether something is allowed or not, like spit-roasting a whole pig over an open fire or challenging someone to a duel during a team huddle, just don't do it.

Keep in mind that less is more. We'll cover this further in chapters on writing emails and delivering presentations, but remember that people with direct communication styles greatly appreciate reading and hearing messages that are succinct and to the point. As I stated earlier, this style may be difficult to master for those of you whose cultures encourage detailed explanations of research before driving a point home, but I want to repeat this concept because as you'll come to see, you can quickly be labeled long-winded, unnecessarily verbose, or boring if you don't state your main conclusion at the outset.

Always be on time—or early. People at several companies I work for chuckle about how there's the real time when a meeting should start, say 10 AM, and their company's time, which is maybe ten minutes later. My advice on this is to always be there at the real time no matter what the company time may be. Who knows—maybe the one time you decide to arrive at a meeting on "company time" could be the time when, for whatever reason, everyone else—including your boss—shows up at the real time. You don't want to be the only latecomer; it doesn't send a good message. By the way, know that meeting start times may vary within a company too. If you transfer from Software Development to Internal Security, for instance, you may find out that the security people double-lock the doors one second after the meeting start time.

. . . .

The 50-Minute Meeting

Some companies are now scheduling meetings for 50 minutes instead of 60, so people can have time to travel to their next meetings. If your company doesn't allow this grace period, and you know you'll be a few minutes late to a meeting, email or text the meeting organizer to say exactly when you'll arrive and why you're running late. If a meeting runs late, always try to email or text the leader of the next meeting, indicating your situation.

. . . .

There are many more smart ways to communicate things about yourself, as we'll talk about in upcoming chapters. Remember that your coworkers and peers are a good reference point for you about how you can understand company norms (not that your peers will always get it right). Observe what they do and how they do it. Consider how others react or respond to coworkers when they behave a certain way. Learn by watching and listening.

Some people are good at communicating things about themselves in certain contexts but not in others. Your best work friend in the next cubicle may show up early for every meeting, but you may notice that she hands out ultra-thick presentation decks full of pages composed in a tiny font, and after she starts to speak other people quickly grow restless (as communicated by checking emails, staring into space, or sleeping with their eyes open). Perhaps she hasn't mastered the less-is-more lesson.

Over time, people will form a particular impression of her, which will affect the way they interact with her and how effective they think she is at her job. When someone is in line for a promotion, would she be considered over someone else who might represent themselves better in meetings? Who knows? But everything she does communicates something.

And everything you do does too.

What to Wear

When I was entering seventh grade, the all-boys school I was about to attend had just abandoned its long-standing tie-and-jacket dress code. This was in the late 1960s, when traditional American prep schools were deciding whether to adapt to a new normal. Of course, my classmates and I were thrilled that we didn't have to wear a restrictive uniform the way our friends at the old-fashioned schools still had to do.

Instead, we were able to express ourselves by our garb. The "uniforms" we chose for ourselves labeled us immediately: slackers, druggies, nerds, jocks, poor kids, rich kids, etc. Though looks aren't everything, we knew that our choice in clothes made a statement about who we were, what we were into, or who we aspired to be. This is not news for anyone who went through adolescence. I'm sure you also fretted about which jeans, tops, jackets, shoes, backpacks, and hairstyles would either help you blend in anonymously or stand out to make a point.

To a certain extent, this same thinking also applies to how you dress and present yourself at work. Whether you wear jeans or a suit and tie, you're communicating something about yourself. A man wearing a suit and tie may communicate professionalism, but he might seem out of place if everyone else, including his boss, dresses in jeans. A coworker wearing a tank top and a lot of chains who sports a large tattoo of a skull on his bicep might stand out in a traditional corporate setting but fit right in at a factory. A peer who shows up for an important client meeting wearing shorts might communicate a lack of care or respect unless everyone received the Today Is Shorts Day memo, you're in Bermuda, or the client is a shorts manufacturer and you're wearing its highest-end pair.

If your job requires you to wear a uniform of some kind, you don't have to agonize about your couture choice. Customer service workers, firefighters, lifeguards, medical professionals, and clowns, for example, are often expected to look the part, which means they won't necessarily be judged for their choice in clothing. (Well, I do always judge clowns.)

But even if you have to wear a uniform, you still have a choice about how the rest of you comes across. Is your hair a mess? Do you wear green lipstick? Have on clown shoes?

I'm all for individuality. But you have to make a choice about the extent to which you want to conform to the culture of your workplace or the surrounding city. Would you feel most comfortable wearing what most others do? Will you feel comfortable donning the traditional jeans-and-hoodie look of Silicon Valley, the khakis-and-black-fleece-vest-with-logo look at hedge funds, the tailored-suits-and-expensive-dress look at high-end private wealth firms, or the polka-dot-and-baggy-pants look at clown conventions?

And how important is it for you to deviate from the norm and try to stand out in some way? It's sort of like being an adolescent again.

In the workplace, I'd boil down your choices of clothing to three classifications: informal, business casual, and business formal.

For guys, informal usually offers a lot of freedom (assuming what you're wearing is clean): any kind of shirt (but no T-shirts with offensive words or phrases, please) and jeans. Ask coworkers to find out whether shorts or flip-flops are allowed. Business casual means wearing a nicer (clean) shirt, (clean) trousers, and respectable shoes. It would be good to make sure your clothes aren't overly wrinkled or faded. And business formal means wearing a suit and tie and shined shoes. A quick check for nasty stains may require a trip to the dry cleaner.

Many women claim that business formal and business casual are sort of the same thing these days; there's no middle ground. Honestly, I would give the same advice to women as I give to men: your clothes should be clean and non-wrinkled; your shoes shouldn't be scuffed; and you should feel that you are dressing appropriately based on the context that best applies to your situation. If you work in a place that still specifically dictates in a multipage manual what type of attire is appropriate for women, you may want to find out if that company also dictates what it considers appropriate behavior for women. I can't make decisions for you, but I put up a big red flag if I hear that someone wants to work at a company that has old-fashioned rules and discourages individuality.

As I mentioned, when choosing your styles of dress, remember to ask yourself the following questions and develop your own sense of style based on your answers:

- What is the location of my work?
- What is my professional level (or the one I aspire to)?
- Is my job client-facing?
- What is everyone else in the company wearing?
- How do I want to come across to others?
- Would I feel that I'd lose my sense of individuality at this company?

. . . .

Acceptable and Not-So-Acceptable Attire

Some items that are perfectly appropriate in the workplace:	Yarmulkes, hijabs, and turbans.
Some items that are inappropriate in the workplace:	Tutus, swimwear, and pajamas. (There are, of course, always exceptions to the rule, like if you dance for a ballet company, work as a lifeguard, or model pajamas for a living.)
Some items that no one at work should see:	Any part of your underwear (or anything that it should be covering). Also, oozing sores. Definitely no oozing sores.
Items that you should be aware of:	Tattoos and piercings, even though they are much more socially acceptable today than they were in the past. Note that if your tattoos and piercings are visible, people will often wonder about them: what they represent, how extensive they are, whether they hurt, why you had them done there. Truly, you don't have to explain anything to anyone, but depending on the industry, know that some businesspeople think tattoos and piercings are unprofessional. My advice is to consider covering up tattoos (or removing piercings) if you're invited to attend a client meeting and think you may distract people from the task at hand. If you're not sure how acceptable your tattoos or piercings might be, ask a coworker or manager before the event.

. . . .

Some days, I'll look at my calendar and see that I'm working in the morning for a client with a super-casual dress policy and in the afternoon for a business formal client. In that case, I'll wear a suit without the tie to the morning client and take off my suit coat and put the tie on for the later meeting. Of course, no one at my morning meeting would care if I had a tie and suit coat on or not, but I don't want to call attention to my clothes.

You're definitely allowed to show your sense of style, but look around to see whether your work clothes are within an accepted range of your company's sartorial norms.

The Color Purple

Dear Someone Else's Dad,
Is it a bad career choice if I were to dye my hair purple?
Thanks,
Luv My Hair

Dear Luv,
You can dye your hair any color you want. Just know that some people—supervisors, coworkers, clients, and customers—will think of you as the person with purple hair and, depending on the context for where you work, treat and interact with you the way they think they should interact with a person with purple hair. Purple hair doesn't mean you won't be brilliant in your career, but be prepared for some people to "get it" and others not to. In the end, you need to decide how you want to balance being true to yourself and being the best you can be in your specific work scenario.

What's That Smell?

Dear Someone Else's Dad,
I don't want to just look good at work; I want to smell good too. What do you think of wearing cologne or perfume on the job?
Thanks,
Sweet One

Dear Sweet,
There's nothing wrong with smelling nice, but I recommend keeping scents to a barely noticeable level. You don't want people to know you're coming down the hall because your fragrance makes an appearance before you do. Also, you don't want your office space to have a distinctive odor (positive or negative) so that after people leave your area, others say, "Hey, you must have been hanging out in Kai's office!"

How to Greet People

I travel a lot and enjoy learning how people greet strangers, coworkers, and clients in business settings around the world. In New York, where I'm from, "How are you?" "How's it going?" and "Howya doing?" are greetings that don't require more than a "Fine, thanks," "Good, you?" or a "Howya doing?" back without an answer to the first question. No one is truly looking for a substantive answer. As much as you feel you may want to answer how you're really doing, you'll jolt the other person if you say something longer than "Good, thanks," and they may not pay attention anyway.

> **Person 1:** Howya doing?

> **Person 2:** Well, the truth is, I'm not doing that good. I

think I had a bad piece of veal that's not really sitting well. My stomach is gurgling a bit, and I'm breaking out in a sweat.

Person 1: Cool! This way to the conference room.

Person 2: (Gurgle, gurgle.)

(Note: If you are legitimately sick, send an email saying you've come down with a bug and hope you can reschedule. Sweating and gurgling your way through a meeting might not only be miserable and embarrassing for you but also prove a distraction for others or cause you to look unprofessional.)

Conversely if you were Person 1, don't be offended if you receive a short, impersonal response ("Fine.") when you greet people first. This fast greeting may not be similar to the way things were at your last job or the way things are where you come from.

In the UK, you might hear someone greet you with "You alright?" (which, if you haven't heard it before, especially when said with a concerned-sounding intonation, might cause you to think that you look like you are on your way to your grave). Again, don't be offended at the question; this is just the cultural norm. An appropriate response would be something like "Yes, thanks. You?" (Then later, you can check your face in the bathroom mirror to make sure you're still among the at least semi-living.)

In the UK, as in many other countries around the world, you greet someone by being nice and asking how the other person is doing; then the appropriate thing for the person to do is to respond simply, asking in turn how you're doing. Answers are always short and simple. In France, if they greet you with "*Ça va?*" respond with "*Oui, ça va.*" In Brazil, if they ask you, "*Tudo bem?*" answer with "*Tudo bom.*" In Italy, when they say, "*Come stai?*" tell them "*Sto bene!*"

I'm sure there'll be exceptions to the rule from time to time, and who knows, you could meet someone who genuinely wants a thoughtful response to a greeting or wants to begin a conversation with you. When I was in Texas once, I asked someone, "Howya doin'?" (I was pretty impressed with myself for droppin' the *g* to fit in with what I perceived as Texas culture), and I expected the standard "Howya doin'?" back from the person. Instead, I got back "I'm doin' great, Peter! How're *you* doin'?" which surprised me, since I've seldom known a stranger to actually care how I was doin', and I didn't originally care that much about how the other person was doin'. I learned to read the cultural cues around me, and now when I'm in Texas, I smile broadly and say, "I'm doin' just great! How 'bout you? Let me tell you about some veal I had."

. . . .

Good Morning!

When you arrive for work at the start of the day in an American company, you will most certainly be greeted with a simple smile and the standard "Good morning," or "Morning," or "How are you doing today?" In my extensive travels, I've seen many different kinds of morning greeting rituals, including one in Buenos Aires where the first meeting of the day always starts with everyone kissing each other's cheeks and hugging everyone and asking how coworkers' evenings were. I admit I was startled by this ritual the first time I was in Buenos Aires for a morning meeting, but also strangely flattered. Never before had anyone I worked with been so excited about how I had my eggs that morning.

. . . .

The Importance of a Handshake and Proper Greeting

First impressions are important when you're greeting someone, so it's critical to have a handshake that says, "This is an appropriate handshake." Some handshakes communicate, "I'm showing how strong and aggressive I am because I'm a business person and a business handshake is firm and . . . Oh sorry, did I just break your fingers?" Other handshakes communicate, "I have poor social skills, and you can probably tell that because my hand feels like a piece of raw squid. Sorry, I'll go hide somewhere." And still other handshakes say, "I went to an exclusive school where old-fashioned manners were drummed into our heads, so I will tip your hand as though I were about to kiss it but just tug on it gently instead."

Here's what I recommend: Look the person in the eye, smile, and introduce yourself, clearly saying your name. Extend your hand for a firm (but not painful) handshake, facing the other person directly. (If you're worried that your hand is too sweaty for a dry handshake, keep some tissues or a handkerchief in your pocket for a quick dry-off before a high-stakes greeting.) Take the other person's hand in a confident, reassuring manner. Lightly pump the other person's hand (not too hard and not too high), maintaining eye contact and a genuine (but not creepy) smile. If it's appropriate to the situation, add a simple "It's nice to meet you," "It's good to see you again," or "How are you doing?" Don't pull your hand away too quickly, but don't hold on to the other person's hand too long either.

Handshakes and proper greetings are important, mostly because you'll stand out (and not in a good way) if you do something outside of the norm. Honestly, accidentally spilling coffee all over the place and making an effort to clean it up may make you feel that you've blown your professional cover. But accidents happen, and people forget about them. Crunching someone's hand and saying, "What's the matter? Too strong for ya?" puts you down several notches on the professionalism meter. Good luck climbing back up.

Bro Hug! Bro Hug!

Dear Someone Else's Dad,

My college friends and I always bro hug when we see each other. I was in a business meeting with one of my buds the other day, so we naturally hugged without thinking about it. Was that wrong?

continued

Thanks,
Adult-Frat Man

Dear Frat,
I wouldn't worry about the hug so much; I actually find it kind of sweet. I just would have said something like "We're best buds from college," so coworkers who were wondering about it would have had a little more context. In a very formal setting—say a board meeting—you may want to do a handshake with a little half hug: lean a bit and perhaps touch each other's shoulders with the other hand. Let's call it the faux bro hug. Always remember to greet people according to the formality of the occasion to maintain the appropriate level of professionalism.

Remembering Names

When the people you're meeting offer their names, say, "It's nice to meet you, Riva, Rafe, Raffi, Rufus, Rafa," shaking the hand of each person as you do. (You don't have to repeat their names all in the same sentence; just acknowledge each person as a show of respect.) Repeating the names out loud can help you better remember them later on. It's not a bad practice to remember peoples' names, not only because you can then refer to people by their correct names and introduce them to others properly, but you'll also really impress everyone if you get their names right. If possible, do a quick mental recap of new names, perhaps even using mnemonics to keep new names straight. For instance, "Riva's from Geneva, Rafa is from Jaffa, Raffi is daffy, and Rufus is a doofus." Actually, don't do that; those are horrible mnemonics.

But you could make a connection between Jerry's brown tie, which looks like chocolate, which is a flavor of Ben & Jerry's ice cream. Or Olivia's green blouse is the color of an olive branch. I know these sound inane, but try it sometime. Just remember not to call Jerry "Ben."

After I meet new people, I try to discreetly jot down their names and details I remember about them, especially where they sit around a table. Sometimes I make notes of what they were wearing and what they said. But be careful what you annotate; it's *guaranteed* that notes like "Rafa— dude with greasy hair and glasses" or "Rufus—teeny tiny weaselly guy; nasty; don't think I like him" will somehow be seen by the wrong person. You don't want Rafa coming up to you later saying, "So I hear you think my hair's greasy, eh? Problem with that? You afraid my grease is going to get all over you?"

Another technique for remembering names is to offer your business card to new acquaintances in exchange for theirs. As they give you their cards, look at their names and back at their faces to link the two in your mind. You could even subtly arrange the cards in front of you in the way people are sitting around a table.

But the best way to get to know someone's name is to actually use their name in conversation. "Thanks, Jo, for preparing the summary." "Ren, can we follow up on that?" "Really appreciate your interrupting me, Lola." (No, don't say that.) You'll usually get immediate eye contact back once you've used someone's name, so that action will also reinforce the name with the face. I do offer two warnings, however: 1) Don't overdo the name thing; "Good point, Raj," "Thanks, Raj," "You know, I was thinking, Raj . . ." since that can be completely annoying; and 2) If you remember someone's name wrong—and keep incorrectly repeating it—you've blown your whole strategy.

If you do get someone's name wrong, they'll almost always correct you and then forget about it after a few moments (unless you said something like "Hey there, Fathead"). Don't worry. Most people don't mind that much, and you can politely apologize. And there's no need to feel overly embarrassed and berate yourself for a simple mistake, turning your face against a wall when you see them, or running and hiding in a bathroom stall and waiting until they leave the building. Similarly, be gracious if someone gets your name wrong. It happens. And part of being a professional is your ability to demonstrate your patience, understanding of what's most important, and willingness to build bridges with people. Still, if someone called me Fathead . . .

Here's a good idea: look up the people you'll be meeting in advance on LinkedIn. Most people have a picture in their profiles, so you can match the names and faces before you meet them. If they don't have a profile picture, you could do a little more Google sleuthing to find a picture. You may learn an interesting thing or two about them; just don't be too creepy about it. Remember to be cool when you meet them. There's no need for, "I've been wanting to meet the big hot-dog-eating champ, and now here you are!"

I Have a Nickname for You

Dear Someone Else's Dad,
I work with two people named Pat; one is male, the other female. I started referring to them as Pat the Man and Pat the Girl and got some eye rolls. Anything wrong?
Thanks,
Bill The Guy

Dear Bill The . . .
Yes, and if your name were also Pat, I'd call you Pat the Dummy. Even if you checked with the Pats, and they agreed to those nicknames, which I doubt they would, other people might be offended that you refer to one as "man" and the other as "girl." It would be more professional to use their last-name initials to distinguish them (e.g., Pat R. and Pat G.). If they're both Pat G., use their full names for clarity. Don't give people nicknames; let them decide what they should be called.

And What about Your Name?

Some people are thrown off by names they have never seen or heard before, so these names may occasionally be difficult for coworkers to know how to pronounce. If you have a name that people seem to struggle with and you prefer to go by a nickname, let people know early on: "I know it's a hard name to pronounce, so please just call me Ritt," or "Actually that's my last name you're using—I know it's confusing. Feel free to call me Jin." If you don't go by a nickname but have a difficult-to-pronounce name, try a direct but polite approach, patiently explaining how to say your name and articulating it clearly so others can hear you. It's not OK for people to mispronounce your name in meetings or regular everyday interactions, so don't feel bad about gently correcting them until they get it. Let's hope your coworkers are open and willing to learn, the same way you should be for them if their own names are hard to pronounce.

I also want to point out that if you have a name that is gender-traditional, such as David for a male or Anne for a female, and you are the opposite gender, transgender, or gender-fluid, you are under no obligation to explain why your name is what it is. If someone is confused after you've introduced yourself, simply spell it out and leave it at that. Similarly, if you have a name that your parents made up, you can explain the reason if you want (e.g., "My parents always liked the Grateful Dead, so they named me 'Dead.'"), or just leave it alone.

We've talked about how first impressions—your behavior, dress, promptness, and basic etiquette—can almost imprint in people's minds something about you. Of course, over time those impressions may change, but show yourself in the best light when introducing yourself and greeting others. In the coming chapters, we're going to move on to what people think of you when you open your mouth. (Advice #1: Don't drool. Advice #2: Brush your teeth regularly.)

But before we open our mouths, let's focus a bit on the things we do when we're not talking, such as what we do with our hands (hint: don't play with your hair), our eye contact (hint: don't roll your eyes), our mouths (hint: spit out your gum), and our posture (hint: don't cross your arms to show disdain). We'll also discuss how to improve your listening, a skill some consider the most important one in business. Wait, were you paying attention?

You Can Call Me JAMES

Dear Someone Else's Dad,

My name is James Arnold. When someone receives an email from me, the From line says, "Arnold, James," which causes a lot of people who don't know me to respond, "Hi, Arnold." I always write, "Thanks, James" at the end of my emails, and my signature has large block text saying, "JAMES ARNOLD." I still get called Arnold. Any tips?

Thanks,

JAMES

Dear Arnold, James,

Ah, the curse of having first and last names that can be both first and last names. Some choices: 1) You could send the offending emailer a friendly note such as, "By the way, please call me James; everyone does!" The recipient may suddenly realize that she got it wrong before or, if she isn't really paying attention, think you're a wacky guy who likes to go by his last name. 2) You could write, "Didn't you notice that I wrote my name as James and that my signature says James?" (Hey, it's a choice, just not the optimal one.) 3) You can pick your battle and live with it, especially if you're corresponding with someone you'll never correspond with again. 4) You can change your name to Arnold James and hope that people finally call you James.

I'd personally vote for options 1 or 3.

Three

THE UNSPOKEN STUFF

When was the last time you thought, *I just don't like that person, and I don't know why*? Maybe it was because she wore too much eye makeup, or maybe he had his face in his phone while speaking to you, or maybe his voice trailed off at the end of every uttered sentence. How about the person who told an inspiring story with a dreadful monotone in his voice, a sour expression on his face, and a twitch in his sleepy-looking eyes?

Conversely, maybe you had a warm and fuzzy feeling for someone who smiled a lot or someone else who made a point to have very focused eye contact with everyone in a lecture hall.

How did you feel about another person who nodded and smiled as you were talking and then asked a follow-up question that had nothing to do with or even contradicted what you just said?

All of these examples come under the topic of nonverbal communication. We are certainly influenced by words, but we become more or less engaged in words depending on how a speaker behaves when delivering them. In addition, as speakers we become more animated and focused when we know an audience is demonstrating that it is truly engaged in our words.

In the section "What to Wear," I discussed how people make immediate judgments about you before you start to speak. Let's now focus on how body language, eye contact, and vocal quality can be the source of others' positive or negative judgments about you.

It's Not Just What You Say: Nonverbal Cues

Certain nonverbal behavioral cues project different meanings to different people. One person might notice a speaker inadvertently scratching his face and automatically be reminded of a dreaded tenth-grade teacher who always scratched her face right before she yelled at the class. Another person will see the face-scratching and be reminded of a *Seinfeld* episode where Elaine scratches her face while talking about the good time she had on a trip until Jerry points out that face-scratching-while-talking equals lying.

Some people will think of the dude who puts his shoes up on his desk as super cool for being so relaxed. Others (me) associate the gesture with a complete full-of-himself jerk. Middle Easterners and people from certain Asian cultures like Thailand view the behavior as rude and disrespectful. Different strokes for different folks.

I'm going to break down nonverbal communication into two types: 1) visual cues, what people see; and 2) vocal cues, what people hear.

Visual Cues

By visual cues, I mean what people are looking at when you're speaking, whether it's what you wear, how you stand, or the way you uncontrollably start to dance a jig whenever someone says, "Good point." The goal for all of us is not to distract others with weird behavior, like jig dancing, but instead use our body language and eye contact to enhance our messages.

Your Body Language

Whether you are standing in a manager's doorway, approaching a group, sitting at your desk, or presenting on a stage at a conference, people will notice how you carry yourself and may make unfair assumptions about you based on what they see. Let's break down what people are looking at and how to make sure your physical presence is professional and appropriate.

Standing Postures

When you are just hanging out in the office—standing around casually— no one is really focusing too much on how you're standing unless you con- sistently and continually scratch your back against the copier machine or suddenly start to hop around like a bunny and ask for carrots. But let's say the casual hanging out suddenly becomes a bit more formal when a client walks in and stops to chat. Your stance (or bunny hopping) may commu- nicate something, even if you're doing something you're not aware of, like standing with your arms crossed.

Standing with crossed arms doesn't necessarily label you as a specific type of person, but some people, based on what they've been taught or experienced firsthand, might think you're coming across as defensive or closed. Hey, you could just have been cold and were crossing your arms to keep warm, but others who encounter the sight of you in that posture wouldn't necessarily know that.

Think about the nerve-wracking situation when you're standing alone in the middle of a stage as you're presenting to a large crowd. You're think- ing, *Should I plant my feet or walk around? Where should I put my hands?* There's a lot to think about before you open your mouth to speak.

The best practice for a formal stand-up presentation is to stand com- fortably and solidly, feeling that you're completely stable from the hips down. Raise both hands close to your body at mid-chest level and hold one hand in another or slightly hold on to one thumb. This should feel awk- ward. Good. To your audience, boss, crowd, etc., you look professional. In this posture you are essentially putting a frame around where the good stuff is coming from, where the top of the frame is the top of your head and the bottom of the frame is your almost-connecting hands. You're basically telling people, "Don't look below my arms; there's nothing interesting going on down there."

No, you don't have to stand there like a statue. As you become more comfortable, your barely touching hands will start to gesture naturally based on what you're saying. You also may find that you'd like to move a bit. Fine, go ahead if there's a reason for it (you want to sit in a nearby chair; you want to cross the stage to answer a question for a different part of the audience; your feet hurt; you suddenly decide you need to demonstrate a cool dance step you saw on *Dancing with the Stars*). But remember to stop and plant your feet again.

Here is a list of some stances and postures, possible interpretations of those behaviors, and potential reasons why a person may have stood that way.

Stance/Posture	Possible Interpretation	Why a Person Might Be Doing It
Hands on hips	Bossy, annoying, jerky, like they are talking down to you	Clueless that hands are on hips
Arms crossed	Hiding something, cold, likes hugging self, untrustworthy	Clueless that arms are crossed
Wandering back and forth, looking at the floor	Looking for loose change, examining carpet cleanliness	Completely nervous and unsure of how to channel the nervous energy
Rocking	Making me dizzy, idiot	Clueless about rocking
Hands in pockets, loud jingling of change	Sudden craving for ice cream	Not schooled in the impoliteness of hands in pockets
Leaning into one hip and then to the other	Showing off flexibility	Very self-conscious about standing in front of others

Keep in mind that my advice on professional stance was for a formal stand-up presentation. You don't have to be so formal when you're speaking to colleagues in a huddle. But you could do a modified professional stance if you're standing in the doorway of your boss's office. Imagine you're holding stuff in one arm. You could plant your feet, stand up straight, and gesture with the free hand.

Sitting Postures

Most of the time in office settings, you'll be sitting at a desk or table or in a chair in a manager's or coworker's office rather than standing on an empty stage. Bad seated posture can be just as evident when you're sitting at a conference table during a meeting. Think about how you may have come across in that situation. Were you slouching, leaning to one side, or sliding down so far that your head was close to the seat? Did you look bored or exasperated? Did you go one step further than the dude with the feet on the table by taking off your shoes?

Here's what I consider the best practice for sitting posture at work: first adjust the height of your chair if possible so your upper torso is clearly visible. I always associate low-sitters as people who like being at the kids' table ("Mommy, I can't reach the chips!"). Sit at the edge of your chair with your feet flat on the floor. Put your forearms against the edge of the table so your hands are in front of you rather than in your lap. This position will ensure that your hand gestures will be from side to side, which will not be distracting.

I recommend not putting your elbows on the table because you might eventually gesture in front of your face. (My wife does this sometimes in dark, noisy restaurants, and I can neither hear her nor read her lips. Hmm. Maybe it's intentional.)

Here is a list of some things people do when they're sitting in a meeting, possible interpretations of those behaviors, and potential reasons why a person may have done those things.

Behavior	Possible Interpretation	Why a Person Might Be Doing It
Slouching	Disrespectful, tired, uncaring, inattentive, lazy	They are clueless that slouching looks bad.
Playing with or twirling a pen	Nervous energy	They automatically pick things up without thinking.
Placing feet on the table	Disrespectful, too casual, a complete jerk	They are disrespectful or a complete jerk.
Manspreading (sitting with legs spread and taking up two seats on a bench or couch)	"I'm king of the world." Disrespect for other people who have nowhere else to sit.	They learned it from another manspreader.
Spinning in their chair	That's the behavior of an eight-year-old.	They're really eight years old. Wait! How did they get through security?

Some meetings take place in a less formal area with lounge chairs and couches. This is an invitation to sit more comfortably, but I'd recommend following basic norms, like sitting up straight, crossing legs only if others are doing so, and not sitting in the boss's favorite mohair-upholstered, diamond-encrusted chair.

The boss's chair brings me to my final point about seating: where to sit at a conference table. Unless you are running the meeting, I'd stay away from chairs at the ends of the table. If you're scheduled to present something, or are at least expected to speak, take a chair in the middle of either side. If it's just going to be you and one other person, seat yourself at the last chair on either side so the other person has the option of sitting next to you at the head of the table or directly across from you. And unless you're working together on a physical document or on one screen where it would make sense to sit next to another person, feel free to sit one chair away from another person, especially if you're in a conference room that seats a lot of people. You both want to feel comfortable in your personal spaces.

The Body Language of Others

Now that you understand a little about your professional presence and how it affects others' perceptions of you, let's think a moment about reading others' body language, especially when you're the one who's speaking.

Most people at work are polite and not out to hurt your feelings. Imagine that you're at a conference table where you're speaking about your research findings. You think all is going very well—your message is clear, your posture is terrific, your voice is strong—until you look up and see your manager either checking her phone, having a private chat with someone, or sleeping. Your mind has now switched from excitedly presenting your research findings to nervously wondering what you just did wrong to cause your manager to stop paying attention. Your mind is racing: *Did I totally blow it? Will I ever be asked to speak at a meeting again?* Since you've lost your focus, your nonverbal communication starts to falter—maybe you've started to add a lot of "ums" or slouch down in your chair. Your mind is spinning like crazy, and maybe the room is too.

Body language and nonverbal behavior is really a two-way street between speaker and listener. Since you interpreted her behavior in the worst way (disengaged, bored, angry, whatever), you lost your confidence (and maybe your consciousness). The great nonverbal communication you displayed at the outset was quickly diminished after you became aware of the bad nonverbal communication of your listener. When you're speaking, try to monitor others' body language, which may trigger how you respond.

Here are a few other audience behaviors and messages they could convey.

Their Body Language	What This Could Mean	But It Could Also Mean
Yawning	You're boring me; get out; stop talking.	I'm a bit tired, but no big deal.
Turning away from you toward their computer screen	You're boring me; get out; stop talking.	Wanted to check a quick notification, but I'm still paying attention.

Standing up, smiling, and/or escorting you to the door	You're boring me; please get out; stop talking.	I got your point, but I have another meeting now.
Rolling eyes	Your point is inane.	There's a speck in my eye that I'm trying to get out by rolling my eyes.
Suddenly singing "Crazy in Love"	I'm a psychopath.	I really am a psychopath.
Bolting the door and putting up a "Keep Out" sign	Self-explanatory	Mind your own business, please.

When I'm speaking to a crowd, I feel that part of my job is to be more interesting than what's on their phones, to keep people awake without resorting to singing "Rolling in the Deep," and to respect their time. If I see behavior that suggests someone is not listening, I'll automatically change what I'm doing to get them to pay attention. For instance, I may ask the crowd a question (or if I'm feeling vindictive—a rare occurrence, honestly—I'll ask the offending party a direct question) in order to engage the audience more. Sometimes I'll even say, "I don't want to take up any more time, so let me quickly reiterate my main point."

Be aware of others' nonverbal communication so you can assess what mood people are in at the outset and how you may have to adapt as you approach them, whether your assumptions of their behaviors are valid or whether you're being a bit paranoid, and how your nonverbal behavior is affected by others.

Eye Contact

You'll be perceived as honest and credible when having a conversation with colleagues if you establish good eye contact with them. If you're chatting one-on-one with a person, good eye contact doesn't mean staring down the other person without blinking, which would seem kind of freakish and off-putting. A guideline might be balancing 80 percent of your eye contact with 20 percent wiggle room for looking away to ponder something when you're speaking. When the other person is speaking, 100 percent of your time should be spent looking at the other person's face (not to search for moles or food remnants) to focus on the message the person is conveying.

Here are some things to keep in mind:

· If you're in a conference room with multiple people, make sure to give everyone you're speaking to a good share of eye contact. The tendency is to look solely at your manager or key decision maker, but try to develop eye-contact relationships with everyone in the room. I don't want to make the amount of time per person a rigid number, but you should feel comfortable with a few seconds per person before moving on to another person.

· If you're with people who aren't giving you eye contact, perhaps they are looking at their screens. Don't automatically think that they won't look up. Keep your eye contact focused on them just in case you say something ("Want to hear a story that's really disgusting?") that will get them to look up at you. Always be prepared for them to make eye contact back.

I often say the keys to a speaker's perceived credibility with an audience relates to her strong eye contact and strong voice (we'll talk about voice in the next section). Imagine talking to some woman who looks only at your neck and speaks so softly or mumbles so much that you can barely decipher the words. You could assume that she is lying—a lot of people think liars can't look you in the eye—and is uncertain about her message; after all, why isn't she speaking up? Later, you may read your notes from this meeting, do some research, and discover that the woman was a total genius. Unfortunately, her poor eye contact led you down the wrong credibility path.

Conversely, you could be speaking with a guy who makes great eye contact with you and speaks with a strong voice, using interesting inflections to support his points. *Wow,* you might think, *this fellow is super confident. I'm going to believe every word he says.* Let's say when you look at your notes from this meeting and check some of this guy's facts, you realize he was a total fraud. Hmm.

Hello? Anyone Out There?

Dear Someone Else's Dad,
I was once told that if I make a speech to a large crowd, I should look out over their heads and kind of scan back and forth. Won't that hurt my neck and make people realize I'm not actually making eye contact with them?
Thanks,
Eye Scanner

Dear ES,
With large crowds, you should try to make eye contact with as many people as possible, but don't do it by scanning. (Plus, you don't want to give yourself whiplash.) Instead, focus on some people in one part of the audience for a bit, then gradually change your focus to people in an adjacent section. You can physically move across the speaking area, stop, and do the same with people on the other side of the auditorium. As you look at each section, you'll very likely find a few friendly, smiling faces, which are perfect ones to focus on. You'll demonstrate effective, focused eye contact, and your neck should be fine.

Facial Expression and Attitude

I'm a big fan of authenticity, so I want to temper my comment about facial expression a bit. First, I like to spend my workday with people who have pleasant demeanors and smile appropriately, especially when I smile at them. Second, I appreciate seeing someone's facial expression and attitude match the mood of the message: enthusiasm, excitement, disappointment, etc.

If you're a naturally bitter or angry person and show your bitterness and anger in your face all the time, I've got to be honest: I don't want to spend a lot of time with you. On the other hand, if you're a super cheery person whose facial expression constantly exudes perkiness and joy, as much as I like the optimism, I might find you a tad exhausting, especially when I'm in deep-focus mode.

But if authenticity is so important, should you just come across naturally and authentically angry/bitter/overly cheery? Here's where it's hard: I don't recommend that people change their personalities, nor would I ever recommend smoothing out some quirks that make us unique. But extreme attitudes at work won't get you far. (Save it all for your life outside the office, and see where it takes you.) I recommend trying on a pleasant demeanor and facial expression. You can definitely show some emotions when they hit you, but those emotions shouldn't define you at work.

I hate to sound like the message in a cheesy greeting card, but smiles do go a long way. And honestly, so does a generally positive attitude. I work with many human resources professionals who give me the rundown of the people I'll be working with. They might say, "Here's one to watch out for," which often is followed by something like "seems difficult," "can't tell whether feedback is getting through," or "don't get a sense whether this person is engaged in work here." Very often the reason for the negative comments revolves around observed behaviors, like having a sullen face or not showing enthusiasm.

As I said, don't put on a fake, plastic smile—people can see right through phoniness—but try to demonstrate through actions, words, and demeanor that you are committed to the work you've been assigned.

Vocal Cues

In a multicultural workplace, it's very common to hear people speaking English with different accents. I actually enjoy going to meetings (most common when I work in London) where everyone at a conference table pronounces words slightly differently. (I also bemoan the fact that my fluency in other languages is pitiful.) An accent often adds a bit of natural timbre to someone's voice, which makes me pay attention more than I would if I were listening to a bunch of people who speak in the same dull monotone.

In fact, when I ask seminar participants what makes a speaker boring, usually the first comment is something about a dull voice. We can't control how our own voices naturally sound, and we all detest listening to our voices on a recording. ("I really sound like *that*? How awful!") But we can control some things that can make our voices complement and enhance what we're saying. These include volume, rate, articulation, and inflection. We also can legitimately rid ourselves of annoying fillers such as "like," "you know," "um," and "sort of."

Volume

As I stated in the section on eye contact, a strong voice and good eye contact together are a great sign of perceived credibility. In other words, you could speak in gibberish, but if you look people in the eye and speak with a loud voice, your audience will think you're amazing. Not really, but it's a start.

Many people I work with from Asian countries, especially women, have a difficult time trying to keep their voices at a volume considered as baseline normal in the US. I definitely understand and respect cultural differences and norms, but I encourage people to think about their audiences. In America, where confidence is partly measured by a strong voice, I recommend trying to pump up the volume when the stakes are high. Those situations can include:

- When you have to make a persuasive pitch
- When you're on a conference call, and others cannot read your lips
- Any meeting with higher-ups or customers

Here are some tips to help you add volume to your speech:

- Relax. If you're too tense, you might clench your throat and clog your airflow, which can make your voice too soft.
- Support yourself from your abs. Having a strong core helps your diaphragm produce a fuller sound.
- Imagine speaking to an imaginary person who's on the other side of the farthest wall.

I should balance this conversation by mentioning problems with loud talkers. Loud talkers I've worked with often tell me that they've grown up in big, boisterous families and the only way to be heard was to speak at the top of their lungs. Having a naturally strong voice is a gift for auditorium public speakers, but I hope those people recognize that booming voices in a normal office setting can be off-putting. In meetings, an overly loud voice can come across as domineering and confrontational, which doesn't play well in a working team.

A lot of people with loud voices don't even realize they're speaking louder than normal. Bringing volume down is mostly a physical process that can be helped by seeing how your voice "looks" when you record yourself. Most phones have a recorder function where "blips" are higher or bigger when a voice is louder. A good test is to record yourself and watch how high the blips go when you speak at a normal volume. Try to see what physical adjustments you can make to make the blips a bit smaller. This is not a bad test for low talkers, too, to get them to speak louder.

Rate and Articulation

I hate to be labeled as a "fast-talking New Yorker," even though I am one. Because I am aware of this, as well as its impact on others, I try desperately to slow down my speech when I'm in meetings or conducting lectures. I want people to focus on my words and their meaning so they're not distracted by my method of delivery. To help me slow down, I quietly take a deep breath and focus on enunciation—I literally become hyperconscious of how my mouth and teeth are forming words.

If I do speed up a bit, I still want to ensure that every word is articulated clearly. Speaking clearly is particularly important on phone calls. In a global workplace where we all say words a bit differently, it's important for everyone to slow down and articulate well so others can get used to accents.

If you're concerned about your articulation and speed, record yourself speaking impromptu. (I advise not reading something aloud because some people are lousy speech readers.) When you play it back to yourself, write down the words that are slurred and then spend a few minutes breaking the words into syllables. Say the slurred words again, but this time, pronounce all the syllables clearly. Keep practicing this until you hear a difference.

Filler Words and Phrases

Most of us get stuck once in a while when we're speaking, so we tend to throw in sounds like "ah," "um," and "uh" because we're afraid of the silence that would occur if we didn't fill in the space with something. We use these fillers as transitions or ways to buy us time until we can collect our next thoughts.

It may not feel like it, but the amount of silence that you'd actually allow if you didn't say "ah," "um," or "uh" would probably last about a second or two at most. And a second or two of silence is not necessarily always a bad thing. There are natural pauses in talking, and these can allow a listener to digest the information you've given them.

I do worry, though, when someone can't speak without uttering these filler words—"ah," "um," "uh," or even "like" or "you know"—in every sentence. If overused, they cause a speaker to sound unprepared, unpolished, or unprofessional. The filler words can distract the listener, drawing attention away from the real message. When fillers are repeated enough that they become a pattern, I often find myself waiting for the next utterance rather than listening to the content. ("Did you catch that? He said 'um' five times. Wait, make that six.")

Filler phrases like "sort of" and "kind of" can be particularly irksome, since they're not definitive and can dilute a message. "We kind of met the client the other day and had sort of a nice chat." I don't know how you can "kind of" meet someone, but I'm dying to find out. Overusing "sort of" and "kind of" can also make you kind of sound indecisive or sort of unsure, which, in a kind of a workplace setting, sends sort of a message of being kind of ineffective. Got that?

Here are some other filler words that are unnecessary and a bit overused:

· **"Literally,"** as in "We literally all had breakfast together" or "She literally had the best time."

· **"Yeah, no"** or **"No, yeah,"** as in "Yeah, no, we finished the report" or "No, yeah, I'll take care of it."

· **"Essentially,"** as in "Essentially, we are planning an event next month" or "Essentially, the client was pleased."

Know what filler words or phrases pass through your lips a lot. You can either ask colleagues to be honest with you about what they hear, or if that sounds too embarrassing, record yourself in private speaking completely extemporaneously about something. When you watch the video, try not to be hypercritical about how much you hate your hair/nose/eyes/voice and instead focus on filler phrases you hear. Then be determined to rid yourself of that habit.

Here are a couple of tips:

· Develop strong eye contact. When you look directly at people as you're speaking, instead of looking down or around, you'll be less likely to say "uh" because, let's face it, it's awkward to look at someone directly and say "uh."

· Concentrate on how you form words with your mouth and teeth. If you focus on that area, you'll be less likely to allow yourself to form phrases such as "like" or "you know."

· Don't pressure yourself to get rid of your fillers immediately. Test it out by having a five-minute chat with someone and trying your best to focus on not saying "um," or "you know" for that limited time. You might find the exercise exhausting, but you'll be very conscious of how to rid yourself of the habit.

Affectations

Affectations are ways people recite sentences. Imagine encountering someone repeatedly speaking with a phony accent or in an unnatural manner. Hearing "Oh my dee-ah, I am sooooh disappointed to hee-ah that DREAD-fully awful news as I was sipping my tea!" from a truck driver may sound a tad incongruous and make you spend a few minutes wondering where that affectation came from.

Other affectations are cultural: one person speaks in a certain way, then another follows along because the speech starts to sound normal to them. To the rest of us, however, it may sound weird and label this as juvenile and silly.

Here are three affectations that can have an effect on what people may think about you.

· **Vocal vanishing.** Some people who aren't accustomed to speaking in a strong voice, but who try their best, may find that their voices trail off at the end of sentences. "It's really important to do this project because otherwise we won't be able to achieve…" Whoops, credibility lost. "I'm totally psyched to be working on this team because I'll get the chance to achieve…" Whoops, enthusiasm not believed.

- **Vocal fry.** Similar to vocal vanishing, vocal fry occurs when someone trails off but instead of becoming purely softer, becomes softer and raspy. The next time you hear someone sound like she is softly gargling words at the end of a sentence, you've heard vocal fry.

- **Uptalk.** Uptalk is when plain sentences are turned into questions. "I went to the movies?" "And I really enjoyed it?" "I think it's a great thing to do on a rainy weekend?" "I work at Framehouse?" I'm never sure whether the speaker is looking for affirmation. "Yes, you did go to the movies! Yes, you enjoyed it! Yes, you're right! Do you want me to verify that you work there?" Be declarative, not questioning.

I'm sure you have heard other types of affectations that either make you wonder why the person is talking like that or cause you to make assumptions about the person in general.

Something Wrong with Vocal Fry?

Dear Someone Else's Dad,

I'm a twenty-something professional woman who sees a lot of complaints on the internet about vocal fry. My friends and I vocal fry all the time, and we think it's normal. Don't you think complaining about vocal fry is generational and sexist?

Thanks,

Proud Fryer

Dear PF,

It's not my place to tell you to get rid of an accent, change your hairstyle, or stop vocal frying. I agree that older people are probably more put off by vocal fry than younger people. Just keep in mind that a big part of my job is to make people aware that how they sound can color other people's impressions of them. Some

continued

listeners may not notice a vocal inflection at all, while others may think it makes you seem unsure of yourself or makes you appear juvenile and not appropriately professional.

My problem with vocal fry is the same problem I have with any other vocal affectations like uptalk. Once I hear three sentences in a row with the same intonation of affectation, I'm going to start to anticipate hearing each subsequent sentence in the same intonation. As a result, I stop focusing on the message. It's ultimately up to you to decide how you want certain audiences to perceive you.

What's That You Didn't Say?

Here's a summary of your impressions of vocal cues, what might be going on in your mind, and what the speaker might be aware (or not) of:

What You Hear	What You Could Be Thinking	How Aware the Speaker Is
Lots of "um," "you know," "like," "sort of"	I should take a tally of "ums" per sentence	Unaware of how bad it is
Monotone	zzzzzz	Unaware of how bad it is
Can't hear	Can't hear	Unaware of how bad it is
Speaking too fast	Must be from New York	Unaware of how bad it is
Slurring words	Bad accent, drunk	Unaware of how bad it is

Listening to Learn

Get this: different sales training organizations I've worked with tell their seminar participants that, in meetings with new prospective clients, salespeople should spend between 70 and 80 percent of their time listening and only 20 and 30 percent talking. The trainers stress that after "actively" listening to a potential client, the best salespeople can then better demonstrate how their product or service specifically solves the client's problem.

Not all of you will go into sales, but analysts and associates in any company are accountable to managers and clients, which in my mind really is customer service. And how can anyone serve those customers without listening to and understanding what they want?

As a vendor, I'm always impressed during a second or third meeting with a client when people on the client team refer to something I said in one of our previous meetings. It doesn't matter whether they have just read their meeting notes before they saw me, or whether they truly remembered what I said. I just feel happy that they made an effort to demonstrate that they understood me and absorbed whatever it was I'd said before. All of that listening and reflecting leads to a very good working relationship.

I want to use this section to show how to enhance listening skills, a skill most people feel they have, but few have been trained in. It's rare for me to find someone who had to master listening drills in school, where a teacher would tell a long story and afterward ask a student at random to summarize the main points. Imagine the energy and focus that student would have had to use just to get the points right.

By the time people enter the workforce, they have to find their own ways to develop excellent listening skills by eliminating distractions and glomming on to the main points of someone's story. This all requires a high level of focus, which can be exhausting.

Let's remove the distractions you face right now as you're reading this—the YouTube video you're simultaneously watching, the cup of ramen you're slurping, the stifling hot room you're sitting in—and listen up.

Sorry, What Did You Say?

In the middle of my first semester in business school, our marketing professor asked the class to gather in clusters and write down the most important skill we thought we'd take away from our two-year MBA program. Since I had very little business background before I started the program, I was proud of my newly acquired vocabulary of acronyms—which I was sure would serve me well no matter what I was going to do. I told my group it was obvious that understanding some new accounting regulation would be the most valuable skills we'd get from the program. Other people in the group argued that mastering some current management guru's methods of leadership would make us all rich and powerful (this was the 1980s).

As we went back and forth on this, a woman in our cluster quietly suggested that the most valuable skill we would take away from this prestigious two-year MBA program would be learning how to listen.

How to listen? *What an idiot*, the rest of us thought. We did not want to believe that we had taken out a large student loan to attend a program where the most important thing we were going to learn was something we already knew how to do. Our cluster shot her down fast.

Soon the professor tallied all the clusters' responses and seemed a tad disappointed as he looked at what he'd just written on a flip chart. He turned to the class and asked, "Did any group say 'how to listen'?" All hands in my cluster shot up. We won (this was the 1980s)!

We had all been focusing on the hard skills of business without realizing how much the soft skills truly mattered. (Little did I know that my career would take a turn a few years after business school to focus on how to help people with those soft skills.)

We're Mostly Lousy Listeners

We all know how to show we're listening: We look at the speaker, we smile politely, and when the speaker looks back at us, we do one of those knowing nods to accompany the polite smile. Maybe we also do a small "mm-hmm" to get bonus points.

I have a question for you: How many times have you already done that "mm-hmm" listening style today? Think about that boring friend who went into way too much detail about his job selling insurance. Smile, nod, "mm-hmm." How about your mother, who told you one of your third cousins is getting a divorce? Smile, nod, "mm-hmm." Or your spouse, who told you that you never listen. Smile, nod, "mm-hmm."

To show that you're *really* listening, you might say something lame like "I know!" or "Shut up!" or "Jeez!" or "Oh my Gahhhd!" Then to show that you're *really, really* listening, you might ask extremely broad and unspecific questions like "Right, but do you think others would agree?" or "You're on to something; can you tell me more?" or "Is there a simpler way we can express that to others?" or "Good point. How do you think we should follow up on this?"

All of these questions are just more mastery of fakery. They're generic questions to use as follow-ups when you haven't paid attention to one word the speaker has said.

The problem in business is that when we are forced to focus on someone else's boring story, we become distracted by things around us, like our phones and all the amazing things we rely on them for—the rain outside that's going to delay us from getting to our next appointment, the smell of the doughnuts at the reception table, the nice-looking stranger across the room, and the more interesting people we could be talking to instead of the dweeb next to us.

Even though the task may be hard, our goal has to be to remove those "more important" distractions and put our energies toward actively listening to someone whose story, problem, or idea will lead to a good working relationship.

Recognize What Typically Distracts You

Let's work on getting rid of those distractions so we can listen better. The hardest distraction by far is trying to stay away from what's on our phones. I love watching people immediately grab for their phones as soon as someone at a meeting calls for a break. It's like seeing ravenous wolves dive for a piece of raw flesh. I try to listen for drooling and chomping sounds and look for teeth gnashing.

Different people are distracted by different stimuli. I work with some people who say they can't pay attention when they're in a very chilly room. Others say they can't focus when people talk about complex topics. If a speaker says something about food just before lunchtime, I guarantee many people in the room will start looking at their watches. Other typical distractions that can prevent you from actively listening include:

· How much you want to read the text that just pinged

· How often the speaker says "um"

· How the other person's toupee is ridiculously covering his bald spot

· How you're going to spend the weekend

· How much you truly want to understand what's going on, but you worry you're in way over your head

· How you don't ever pay attention

· I bet your mind wandered while you were reading this list.

Here's a good exercise: Do a self-audit to determine what situations, topics, and people make it hard for you to pay attention. Of course, you can't remove all those distractions, but start small: Try your best to focus on what a speaker is saying for three minutes. Anytime you find that something starts to distract you, try to snap back to reality by seeing whether you can paraphrase in your mind what the speaker has just said.

Take Good Notes

There's nothing wrong with taking notes when someone else is speaking; it's not a sign of weakness. You can't be expected to remember everything someone has said. I like asking, "Do you mind if I write things down?" to show that I'm interested in what the other person is saying. You should always ask this question when you're taking notes on your laptop so that the other person doesn't think you're opening it up to play a game or check how your stock portfolio is doing. When you do take notes, try not to take down every word; try to listen in bits or chunks and then write down the summary or conclusion of these mini topics.

Paraphrase What's Been Said

Remember when I wrote how good I feel when clients bring up something I said at an earlier meeting? The good feeling comes from knowing you were heard.

To paraphrase effectively, look at the notes you've taken and put them in an order that makes sense. Perhaps start with the most important point (which might not have been stated first) and enumerate a couple more. If the speaker demonstrated strong feelings about a certain item, use words to show that you heard those feelings.

Here's an example: "To recap, you'd like me to revamp the sales presentation by Friday so we can highlight this year's wins. By next Wednesday you want the team to complete the research on the kitchen sink drain-trap market to see if there are any synergies with our existing rubber eraser manufacturing process."

As you saw in that example, good paraphrasing is not repeating every word back to the speaker. It's recapping the important words, themes, and emotions of what someone has just said.

Good paraphrases often begin with the phrases:

· "So what I hear you saying is . . ."
· "In other words . . ."

- "Just to recap . . ."
- "Just to make sure I've got it . . ."
- "So if I'm hearing you correctly . . ."

You can practice paraphrasing in meetings too. Good opportunities can appear just after one topic finishes and before the next topic begins, before people dash off for a break, and the end of the meeting.

Never underestimate the power of paraphrasing, even during short one-on-one chats or interviews. There are three other benefits:

1. You'll make sure the speaker knows you've been paying close attention.

2. The speaker can clarify any points you didn't get quite right.

3. The other people in the room who weren't paying attention will now hear a nice summary of what's been said.

. . . .

Test Your Paraphrasing Skills

Here are some opportunities for you to try out your paraphrasing skills:

- On phone or conference calls to make sure that everyone got the overall message
- At the end of meetings to recap and define next steps
- After a client or customer states his or her concerns
- With a manager or coworker to demonstrate that you know what you need to do

. . . .

When you master paraphrasing as part of active listening, you'll be able to clarify inconsistent or vague statements, dig deeper into conversations to find out what others need, and develop stronger relationships with people. It's not a bad skill to have.

You Are So Not Understanding

Dear Someone Else's Dad,

I've read your blogs about active listening, and I try to listen very carefully to paraphrase what my manager says so I can follow through on action steps. A lot of the time when I'm 99 percent sure I have the message right and say something like "So in other words . . . , " my boss will look at me, shake his head, say, "Oh, no, that's not it at all," and then say something completely different! I find it odd that he repeatedly does this even after I sometimes literally read my notes back to him. Am I doing something wrong or is he playing with my brain?

Thanks,

Listening Closely

Dear LC,

Oh, no, that's not what I suggest at all. Just kidding. That situation does indeed sound frustrating. I don't want to automatically assume that your manager is playing a head game with you. It might be that after he hears what he originally said when you read your notes back to him, he can hear flaws in his thought process and needs that time to think a bit more clearly and feel comfortable with his decisions. Don't blame yourself. I'd recommend paraphrasing the second time and outlining the new version to make sure that you're getting the true final version. Perhaps you can send him a follow-up email immediately after your meeting so he can see it all in writing.

Four

LET'S GET TALKING

Eventually at work, you'll have to do more than just shake hands, nod, dress appropriately, or be wonderfully polite. You'll actually have to speak. These days, coworkers, even those who sit next to one another, can text or IM all day and not even utter a sentence. *Why bother?* they might think. *I'm getting my work done.*

I often visit offices and feel as though I've walked into a library or mausoleum. It can be so quiet that I can hear the hum of the water cooler a few rooms away. Offices aren't supposed to sound like a free-chicken-wings-with-every-beer-Friday-after-work-blow-out happy hour at the local pub, but I feel I need to mime instead of ask out loud, "Where's the men's room?" to avoid nasty glares. (Don't ask me how I mime it.)

In this chapter, we'll discuss many things to get your speaking skills ramped up: from knowing how to start and keep up small talk and understanding how much small talk is too much for different audiences to how to paraphrase effectively to demonstrate you've been actively listening.

So ready, get set, let's start yakking!

When Small Talk Makes You Sweat

Many people panic when they have to make small talk. Think about being on an elevator ride down to the lobby of your office building with someone from work. Let's say you know this person only slightly. It's awkward and quiet, and you're both aware of each other's presence. Should you break the silence? Do you look unprofessional if you just stand there, clutching papers in front of your face?

The easiest (and most common) thing to do at that moment is whip out your phone to check out something incredibly urgent, like what the current water temperature is in the Sargasso Sea or what some celebrity named her pug. You could also try to engage in conversation, but since you both got on the elevator on the 44th floor, it's a long way down and you don't know if you could sustain a chat for that long. Maybe, you hope, the elevator will stop soon to let a large crowd of people in, separating you from your chat mate.

But no such luck. The elevator doesn't seem to be stopping, and the silence is loud. You realize you should probably say something, which makes you feel sweaty. You also start to notice a nervous twitch beneath your left eye.

Here are a few inane chat ideas you could try:

- "Sometimes I wish we were on a lower floor so I could walk down!"
- "I'm really in the mood for one of those tacos from the truck across the street!" (Don't say this if there's no taco truck across the street because then it would become even more awkward.)
- "Looking forward to the weekend?"
- "I can't believe it's only 10 AM!" (Don't say this if it's not 10 AM, even if you already said the thing about the tacos.)

Each of these statements could get you a polite, knowing chuckle and a predictable return comment like:

- "I know, right?"

- "I love those tacos!"
- "Oh my gosh, totally!"
- "I know! Can I really have been here just three hours already?"

Which will again prompt a polite, knowing chuckle. And maybe even *more* conversation:

- "I could be out of the building in ten seconds!"
- "Ever try the chipotle chicken?"
- "Me too!"
- "I am so ready for a nap!"

You hope that this polite chuckle chat will last all the way down, but you look up and see that you're only on floor 32. How much more can you say about the chipotle chicken? While we all just want to be polite and have a nice, easygoing conversation with someone else, I know people who hate the dreaded elevator ride so much that they suddenly "remember" that they forgot something in their office when they see another person waiting for the same elevator, hold their phone to their ear with an urgent look on their face so they can pretend that they cannot possibly be interrupted to talk with anyone since the call is too important, or pry open the elevator door from the inside with their bare hands and climb out between floors. (I've used the phone technique when spotting a smiling person with a clipboard approaching me on the street, hoping I'll sign their petition. I add to the urgency by yelling into my dead phone line, "Oh my God, no!" The cheery people get scared and get out of my way every time.)

But honestly, elevator small talk—or small talk in general—really isn't so bad. It's a friendly thing to do, you know you're going to have a finite conversation, and the chuckles and "ahas" can take up a good amount of the time. ("They used to serve the chipotle chicken with a sauce I wanted to bathe in!") Learning how to make small talk can also make you seem more engaged at work and interested in your coworkers.

But more often than not, you'll have to keep a conversation going. Let's say you've been asked to meet a client or customer at the reception area and escort her to the conference room where your team will be meeting you.

The first step is to make sure you're going to escort the right person back to the conference room. You look at a person in reception who you think might be your client and say, "Betty?" Make sure you say "Betty" loudly enough, and double-check that the person you're meeting is indeed named Betty. (You actually should confirm you've got the right person; otherwise, you might say, "Hello, nice to see you; please follow me," and you could be escorting the person who replaces the sodas in the soda machine into your conference room where someone has prepared a very nice spread of croissants and smoked fish.)

If you definitely have the right person, and you're walking to the conference room, you realize you should say something. Just don't say something that reinforces that you're insecure and junior, such as:

- "I'm not the administrative assistant, in case you were wondering."
- "My mom has that same dress."
- [Mumble something inaudible.]

If the client is on the extroverted side, she may start the small talk herself, asking a few questions about how long you've been with the team, where you're from, or where the restrooms are. These are stress-free conversation starters, and you should be able to answer them easily. "Three months." "Shanghai." "Just around the corner on the right." Well done.

But if the person is more of a silent type, you're the one who should make the guest feel comfortable and welcome by acting like a gracious host. You may be the first person she has met at your firm, and you and your behavior will give her the first impression of the people who work there.

You also want people to know that you're responsive, easy to talk to, and professional.

. . . .

What's Going On in Your Head Versus
What's Going On in Their Head

What's going on in your head:

- "Oh, my God. The client is going to see that I'm the kid on the team and will blow me off and wait until a more senior person comes in."

- "I have no credibility."

- "She's going to think I don't even speak English."

- "She's going to ask me a hard question, and I won't know the answer."

- "She's going to ask me a hard question, I'll say something stupid, and she'll know I'm a total fraud."

- "What am I going to talk about on that long walk from reception to the conference room?"

What's going on in the client's head:

- "I'm looking forward to the meeting. Let's get started."

. . . .

Three Smart Ways to Start Small Talk

The elevator example had a definite end point: the ground floor. In other cases, like the meeting with Betty the client, you might have to keep the conversation going. In George Bernard Shaw's play *Pygmalion* and the musical *My Fair Lady*, which is the same story with songs, there's a great scene when high-class professor Henry Higgins instructs his formerly low-class pupil Eliza on how to behave in her first test as a newly refined lady at a high-class social situation. He tells her "to keep to two subjects: the weather and everybody's health. That will be safe." I agree with Higgins about the weather, but I'd stay away from health—it can be too personal, sometimes unpleasant, and can lead to TMI. Do you really need to hear about a painful boil?

Let's start with the weather and discuss some other good (and bad) topics for small discussion.

The Weather

I know talking about the weather is cliché, but it's something we all share, and besides, there is always some sort of weather going on somewhere. The topic works well in any season:

· Beautiful weather: "What do you think of this weather?"
· Crummy weather: "What do you think of this weather?"
· Cold weather: "What do you think of this weather?"
· Hot weather: "What do you think of this weather?"

You can follow up with a personal anecdote as long as it's not too personal. ("The warm weather makes me just want to strip off my clothes!" That one's a no.) The easiest way to continue a conversation about the weather is to ask how it has affected people. Bad weather often means bad commutes, which provides another aspect of weather or a person's day you can talk about. ("I heard there was ice on the rail tracks!") Cold weather often means people wear extra layers and new high-tech fabrics. ("Look at these gloves I just got. They're rated down to minus-50 degrees!") Hot weather leads to chats about where people go to stay cool. ("I wish my building had a pool!") The corollaries and follow-ups to conversations on the weather are limitless. ("It hasn't rained like this since my wedding day when the whole thing was scheduled in a garden!") This seemingly cliché topic takes a little of the pressure off you; almost anyone can talk about the weather. ("Some weather we're having, isn't it?")

The Trip

If someone is from out of town, you have automatic small talk about how the person got to your city or office. There should be lots of opportunities to bemoan travel delays, share the names of good local restaurants, or relay any semi-interesting (you can think of something) facts of historical interest in your city. Here are some examples:

- "How was your trip over?"
- "What other meetings do you have here?"
- "What kinds of food do you like? I know of some good places to eat, if you're interested."
- "How much time for sightseeing will you have while you're here?"

Sports and Other Recreation

Another cliché small-talk topic is about a recent sports event. ("That was some game last night!") Full disclosure: I am a fair-weather sports fan, meaning I only get into sports viewing at the end of a professional season— World Series, World Cup, Super Bowl, etc.—so unless there is some sort of front-page news, I usually have no clue what sporting event happened the night before. I generally stay away from sports topics altogether, but if this works for you and someone is responsive to your sports-related conversation starters, go with it.

I often ask where someone is originally from and then try to make some connection about my experience there, maybe leading to deeper chat on recreation, hobbies, or genealogy:

- "I haven't been to Slattsville in about ten years. Do they still have the cable car that goes to the top of that peak where you can take your bike?"
- "You're from Lake Roughit! How much time do you get to spend outdoors?"
- "Old Greystone is one of my all-time favorite cities. I still have family there, unless they died."

Small-Talk Tips

Notice that most of the questions you would use for small talk are not closed-ended or ones that generate one-word answers like "Did you have a good trip?" where the answer could be a simple yes, or worse, no, which means the person is ready to tell you about her rotten airline service, cab driver, traffic delays, hotel checkout, breakfast, etc. You're welcome to say, "Oh, my! What happened?" But then you actually have to listen to a rant, which may start the meeting in a negative way. A simple, "Sorry to hear that. Can I get you coffee, tea, water, or juice?" could suffice.

Make sure you listen carefully and respond to your guest's responses so you both will feel as though you are indeed having a real conversation. If she talks about her recent ski adventure, show an interest by either mentioning a shared experience or asking a follow-up question about her new love of snowboarding. Don't merely go down your list of small-talk questions.

You and your guests all know that at some point your pleasant banter about the dry heat in Khartoum or your shared secret love of Marmite will somehow have to come to an end. The natural end point can come when others enter the room. If your team is going to be late, be respectful of your guest's time. Ask whether they would prefer to start the meeting with you, adding that you can relay certain information to your team later.

Many young people I have worked with have trouble asking questions because they feel they're being intrusive or because they come from a culture where it might be considered rude to pry.

After some practice in real-world small talk, you'll get more comfortable with more topics. A word of warning though: stay away from topics that make people uncomfortable, such as:

- Politics
- Sex
- Religion
- Any topic that can be construed as discrimination against any type of person or group

If another person starts to veer toward any of those topics, you do not have to engage. You can simply say, "Why don't we start our meeting?" If the conversation becomes offensive, you should tell your manager after the meeting and be specific about what the person said.

Final thought: remember that no one loves small talk, but knowing how to keep a conversation going is a skill that will take you far in many areas of life.

- -

Bad Versus Good Small Talk

Your client: "We were able to help the orphaned children with new school supplies and medical care."
Bad small talk response: "I heard it may rain this weekend."
Good small talk response: "That sounds amazing. How did the children react?"

Your client: "I was able to have a little time to visit your lovely museum."
Bad small talk response: "There's a museum here?"
Good small talk response: "I'm so glad you had some time to explore. I'd love to know what you thought."

- -

How to Chide Chatty Cathy

Dear Someone Else's Dad,
I have a client who has taken a nice interest in my career. She's a woman in her fifties, and I'm a woman in my twenties. Our earlier

small talk had been pretty bland, but over time she started to ask a lot of questions about my personal life, which I was initially open about, particularly about how I moved here to be with my boyfriend. Now every time she comes to our office, she asks with enthusiasm about when we're getting married, how we'll handle our careers if we plan to have children, etc. The questions seem intrusive, and in a recent meeting she announced, looking at me, "I think someone will be having a wedding soon!" And I'd never told her anything like that!

Thanks,

Private Polly

Dear PP,

Oh my God, congrats on your wedding! When's the happy day? (Sorry.) You should talk to your client right now, since blurting out something specific about you betrays a confidence. Be careful about putting her on the defensive and making it sound like you're blaming her. Maybe look at the issue as a two-way street. For example, you can say, "When you hinted about a wedding—which I never mentioned—in the meeting, I felt hurt because I try to keep my private life private at work. Can I ask a favor? Can we both agree that we won't share personal stuff we've told each other to anyone else at work?" Then afterward be careful about divulging much when she asks personal or intrusive questions. ("You know, I'd rather not get into personal stuff. Thanks.")

The broader issue here is how much information you want to divulge to anyone about your life outside of work. You may make wonderful friends at the office, but you have to decide how close you feel you can be to a particular person, especially if your close working quarters make it hard for some people to keep secrets. If you're friends with work colleagues on

Facebook or Instagram, your personal life is automatically fair game. It's all about the consequences of the choices you make.

You don't have to build a social wall around yourself. But you could divulge personal information at the appropriate moment for you: tell people after you're engaged; tell people you're going for foot surgery just before you have to take a leave; tell people how you need to take care of an ill relative once you've figured out the best arrangement.

Know Your Audience

If someone asked me to give a very short answer ("You have two seconds to answer this question . . . Go!") to "How do I become a great communicator?" I'd say, "Knowyouraudience." That was me saying "Know your audience" in two seconds.

We learn to modify what we say and how much we say about a topic when we're pretty young and then master the art some time during adolescence when we learn not to tell our parents the gory details of what happened at a high school party, while we tell our friends TMI. In high school and college, we're then taught to explain or write a lot more detail for extra credit on a test. By the time you get to your job, you might have forgotten the art of tailoring your message to an audience at the expense of the idea of getting extra credit. It's time to relearn how to match the message with the audience.

Who They Are

Let's say you came up with some promising findings as part of your research project on alternative energy. You are so excited that you want to tell everyone you see that day all about it: your colleagues, a regulatory group, a competitor, your grandmother, your three-year-old nephew, and a bartender.

Your excitement may get in the way of realizing that you'll have to change the level of detail, technical language, and length of your description depending on whom you run into. The people you encounter may indeed become enthusiastic about your research if you think about how your message relates to or benefits them. As a result, you can adapt your message so that you'd get these responses:

- Colleagues: "Terrific! We can monetize this idea and make a ton of money!"
- Regulators: "Wow! That will make our systems more efficient!"
- Competitor: "You snide self-promoter. Thanks for rubbing it in my face."
- Grandma: "I can brag about my wonderful, brilliant grandchild's success! So there, Mrs. Farbenthal, who brags about her grandchild's big-deal hedge fund!"
- Nephew: "Cool! Wait, what?"
- Bartender: "Another round?"

Attention Span

In the business world, you also need to be able to adapt messages to different audiences by recognizing that some people simply don't have the time to read or listen to all of what you have to say. Here's a completely unscientific chart that segments people into different levels of attention span.

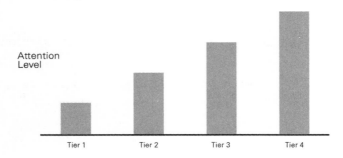

How Much Attention Do They Have?

Think about all the people you communicate with and put them in these attention-span tiers, where Tier 1 people have the shortest attention, Tier 2 more, Tier 3 even more, and Tier 4 people will listen to and read every single syllable you communicate.

What tier people are in has nothing to do with their intelligence or personality. You probably can label some people as clear Tier 1s or clear Tier 4s based on how much attention they pay when you tell them about a detailed work issue. But your Tier 1 colleague may immediately turn into a Tier 4 person when you start talking about another colleague's love life. (Warning: Don't talk about other people's love lives.)

We are all Tier 1 for some bits of information and Tier 4 for others. When you're scanning emails on your phone and you see one that doesn't directly affect you—think "Attention: Carpets Will Be Cleaned This Weekend!"—you may be an automatic Tier 1 for that one. Do you really need to know the type of rug shampoo they'll be using? But you'd switch to Tier 4 if your boss asked you to read the entire email plus the attached PDF file to determine whether the ingredients in the shampoo will affect your highest-paying client, who is allergic to practically everything and will be visiting on Monday.

As we'll discuss later, when you're writing or presenting to multiple-tier audiences at one time, you'll need to satisfy your lower-tier people first by presenting or writing a conclusive message up front, then give more detail to satisfy higher-tier audiences willing to sit in their seats or in front of their screens longer.

There's a lot more to analyzing audiences than just understanding their attention span. But keep in mind that businesspeople will have greater attention spans for your spoken and written word if you can:

- Demonstrate that you understand what their concerns are.

- Relay examples and stories that will resonate with their experience and goals.

- Use the appropriate language based on your relationship (thinking about hierarchy and cultural differences) and on their level of technical expertise.

- Try to figure out what's in it for them.

No One Answers My Emails!

Dear Someone Else's Dad,

I'm an analyst in HR who has to email employees important benefit notices, which have to be opened, read, e-initialed, and e-signed. Sometimes people have to elect certain benefit options on the forms. My response rate is very low, so I have to send out a lot of follow-up reminders. Any ideas on how to get them to respond the first go-round?

Thanks,

HR Pro

Dear Pro,

No offense to anyone who works in HR, but sometimes emails from you can seem scary, especially when you ask people to read a lot of material and make decisions by a certain date. I would imagine that a lot of your recipients might bypass these emails because they require extra time and thought. You can make things easier by creating a subject line to highlight a deadline, writing a first sentence acknowledging that your request will take some time and thought, and crafting bullet points to elucidate the important decisions people need to make. I'd also recommend showing people how your office can help with decisions: holding a seminar with an expert, having a dedicated helpline, or offering to meet privately with people who need to discuss things confidentially.

Remember, too, that emailing someone with "See attached" and a PDF doesn't help time-sensitive email scrollers.

Five

THE RIGHT WAY TO WRITE

The nice thing about the English language is that there are many ways to say the same thing.

- I purchased those two lamps at a department store in Twiddletown.
- In the city of Twiddletown, one can find situated in the town's center an antiquated but still vibrant emporium that peddles a multitude of domiciliary items. It was at that institution that I perused the stock of the lighting department and was enchanted to find these two displayed table lamps, which I immediately procured.

Give me a break. But honestly, which example is easier to understand? While some professionals can be eloquent speakers and beautiful writers, most audiences crave simplicity in messages. Many people I work with often struggle when they're putting together a speech, since they want to use the most impressive, brilliant-sounding synonym for a word like "good." Usually my advice is to stick to the word "good," since it's really what you mean. The audience members aren't sitting there thinking, *Ha, ha, ha. He said "good" when he could have said "first-rate," "superior," "worthy," or "recherché!"*

. . . .

Pardon, I Don't Fathom

I once had a boss who wrote an annual charity solicitation letter that he always asked me to proofread. His concluding sentence one year was "If you're feeling in an eliomosinnary mood this year, I'd appreciate you giving what you can." My reply was "I wouldn't use that big word, since not many people know it just means *charitable*—and you spelled it wrong anyway. It's 'eleemosynary.'" I was being cheeky/slightly obnoxious. I'm not like that anymore. Sometimes.

Even though you now know the correct spelling and meaning of "eleemosynary," don't ever use it unless you're playing some sort of parlor game. Always use words that your audiences will fathom, er, sorry, understand.

. . . .

In this section on writing, I'll provide lots of guidelines on how to think about what your goals are when you write, what audiences need, and how to structure emails and other written communication so they are clear, concise, to the point, well organized, appropriately direct, polite, and professional. We'll also cover how to write longer documents. Along the way I'll give basic reminders on good sentence structure and grammar. I do love good grammar.

All about Emails

Not surprisingly, most writing in business in the US is by email. The only groups that I work with these days that write actual letters that go in envelopes are money managers dealing with very high-net-worth individuals. (Remember how to use envelopes? You lick the flap, and like magic, it creates a seal.) The letters, and in some cases, hand-written notes on personalized stationery, add a very personal touch that many of their clients appreciate.

Throughout the world emails and electronically signed PDFs and Word docs are legally binding. Still, because of time pressure or because emails are sent more and more frequently from mobile devices, people get sloppy writing them. It's not uncommon to see lack of clarity, poor word choices, and inappropriate tone.

Remember that first impressions play a role here too. If your first email to the team stands out in a way that people in your industry or company would label unprofessional or inappropriate, you'll have to work hard to change their impressions of you. Also, your American boss might have forgotten that English isn't your first language, so a couple of minor mistakes in your email might make him wonder what you mean.

I love showing examples of emails that you *wouldn't* want to send at work. As a result, people learn strategies that don't work, see how these emails might affect their intended audience, and know to avoid committing the same mistakes.

Let's go from bad to worse, with lessons on what *not* to do all the way through. Here's a good beginning point:

> Hey HR!
> We defiantly need you guys to do it so we can reach out to our vendor? 😊😊
>
> Thank You,
> MKU
> "You deserve to be good to yourself."—Anonymous

This seems like a simple email, right? How much could a person mess up in so short a message? But there's sloppiness here that can color a person's impression of the sender, diluting her effectiveness as a professional. It isn't a complicated email, but it's important to point out some glaring items. Consider the salutation, for example.

The Salutation: "Hey" is pretty low on the salutation hierarchy list and should mostly be used when you're addressing friends. I don't want to make that sound like a rule though; some companies encourage informality, so "Hey" might be perfectly OK in these organizations. But remember that if you're dealing with clients, customers, lawyers, vendors, etc., who are not as informal as your easygoing colleagues, "Hey" may seem disrespectful. Also, the exclamation point might communicate some false excitement, urgency, or shock. Some recipients may not take the sender seriously.

· ·

Hey Neigh

When I was a kid, my old-fashioned, uber-proper, no-sense-of-humor grandmother would say, "Hay is for horses" whenever one of us said, "Hey!" I couldn't understand why she constantly had to remind us what horses ate every time we were getting another kid's attention.

· ·

· ·

Hierarchy of Salutations

Need a list of different email salutations you can use? Here are some suggestions, going from most formal to least formal:

To Whom It May Concern:
Dear Sir or Madam,
Dear Jan,
Good Morning Jan,
Hello Jan,
Jan,
Hi Jan,
Hey Jan,
Yo Jan,

Hey Bro,
Dude!
Wassup???
[Any kind of snarky, winking emoji]

A lot of younger workers find it difficult to begin with "Dear" because they fear that there's an underlying emotion tied to the word. Believe me, if I wrote "Dear Hari" at the start of an email to you (assuming your name is Hari), the next line would absolutely not be "It's taken me so much courage to finally tell you that I'm in love with you."

"Dear" has always been a formal greeting in written English communication, so don't be afraid to use that salutation in emails when you're introducing yourself, communicating with senior colleagues, or dealing with legal correspondence. Let the other person "Hey" you first, then respond with the same salutation. (Still, I advise against using "Dude" under any circumstances.)

If you're addressing two or three people, you can mention all their names: "Hi Steph, Pat, and Sam." Trouble can arise, though, if Steph, Pat, and/or Sam and other people at your company are status conscious. Sam, as team lead, might be offended to see her name listed last in the To field and in the salutation. Even if you think there are more important things in the world to fret about, I'd recommend playing along and addressing people in alphabetical order or in order of perceived importance.

When you're addressing more than three people, you could address them together with "Hi team," "Good morning all," or even "Hi everyone in Marketing and Sales." As for the status order for a large group, you might want to start with the most senior-level people, alphabetized, followed by the people at the next level down, alphabetized, etc.

· ·

"Hi Ellie," or "Hi, Ellie,"

Some grammar sticklers will write "Hi, Ellie," (with the comma between "Hi" and "Ellie") because that is the correct punctuation you would use if you were writing a sentence. For example, "I walked into the maximum security cell and said, 'Hi, prisoners!'" is grammatically correct with the comma between "Hi" and "prisoners." Today, "Hi" has become a salutation alternative to "Dear," which would never precede a comma (i.e., you'd never write "Dear, Ellie"). As much as I consider myself a grammar stickler, I've adapted to the times and use "Hi Ellie" (without the intervening comma).

· ·

· ·

Salutations in Some Different Countries

Business email salutations in France, Germany, Spain, and Japan are more formal than those in the US. A client in Germany named Helmut Weber will likely not be offended to see an email from Joe in New York beginning with "Hi Helmut." But Joe should be aware that Helmut is used to receiving emails from fellow Germans that begin *"Sehr geehrter Herr Weber,"* which translates to *Dear Mr. Weber.*

If Joe's emails to his client Helmut are written in English, he could demonstrate his knowledge of local norms and use the more formal salutation. Here's a list of some formal salutations in some countries (LN = last name, FN = first name):

Country	Business Salutation	Translation
Germany	Sehr geehrter Herr LN Sehr geehrte Frau LN	Dear Mr. LN Dear Ms. LN

France	Monsieur LN	Mr. LN
	Madame LN	Ms. LN
Spain	Estimado Sr. LN	Dear Mr. LN
	Estimado Sr. LN	Dear Ms. LN
Japan	LN-san	Hi FN
	LN-sama	Dear Mr. LN

Let's continue looking at this email from MKU to HR:

Defiantly. Auto spellcheck is terrific, but you should proofread to avoid having your computer decide that you wanted to write "defiantly" instead of "definitely." There's a big difference in meaning, especially because "defiantly" is such a strong word. The word would puzzle any reader in this context and may make someone email back "Defiantly?"

You guys. Which "guys" is the writer referring to? This is pretty unspecific and also rather casual. Although most young people I work with don't object to the word "guys" as a collective noun referring to people of different genders, I tend to stay away from the term because someone could be offended by it. A more specific phrase like "your marketing team" would be more appropriate and cover a lot of bases.

Do it. Watch out for using unspecified pronouns like "it" in emails because "it" may refer to something the writer talked about months ago, and the recipient could be clueless about what the email is all about.

Reach out. Sometimes "reach out" can require clarification: Do you mean "call," "email," or "text"? I'd be as specific as possible: "Call me at this number tomorrow before noon" or "Text me to let me know a good time to meet."

☺ People use emoticons in emails to soften the tone or express something they don't know the appropriate words for. I see nothing wrong with using a smiley face after a quick "Thanks so much for all your hard work; I really appreciate it" as an extra boost of nonverbal appreciation. However, I'm not a fan of using smiley faces (single or multiple) as a matter of habit because people who repeatedly see emails from you might start to label you "that smiley face guy," and question your professionalism.

I'd stay away from using other emoticons or emojis in business emails because they are perceived as unprofessional. Also, some older business-people just don't "get" emoticons. Finally, many emojis are small, negative, unclear, and have hidden meanings, so I'd hate to have anyone email you back with a "Huh?"

Thank You. Most people close emails with "Thanks," "Best," "Regards," or "Kind regards." The grammatical convention is only to cap-italize the first word, so this email should have ended with "Thank you," not "Thank You."

Here are some other sign-offs you might sometimes see:

- "Cheers"—This is used all the time in the UK as a word meaning *regards*, *thanks*, *pardon me*, and *bye*. Americans really only use the word when they're toasting each other with alcoholic beverages. Since "cheers" is used so much in the UK in emails and not as frequently in the US, some recipients seeing "cheers" automatically assume that the writer is British (or Australian). Don't make your readers overthink things, so don't use "cheers" unless you fly the Union Jack.

- "Love"—Never use this, even if you really like your coworkers. It's not appropriate for a business email.

- "Yours truly"—This is too formal in an American context.

- Just your first name—While this may come across as a bit unfriendly for the first email in a chain, it might work for subsequent ones.

- "Blessings"—It's a good idea to keep religion out of business communication.

- Nothing at all—Use this only after you've had a few back-and-forth emails with one other person and established a level of cordiality in your first few emails.

MKU. I recommend that people sign their emails with the names they liked to be addressed by rather than using initials. (Should I say, "Hi, MKU!" when I see you?) Also, if you've got a long first name that is likely unfamiliar to your audience and you prefer a nickname, make sure you sign your email with that nickname. I've seen people put their preferred nickname in parentheses in their standard signature like "Fyodor (Teddy) Dostoevsky." In the middle of a back-and-forth email exchange with someone, people often sign off with just the first initial of their first name. This practice is considered friendly, and lets the other person know you've developed a rapport.

The funky font and the inspirational quote. Don't do either of those. Someone could create an entire personality profile of you just by looking at that weird font. Whether the assumptions people make about your life are accurate or not, you're showing a personal side of you that should be kept for your personal email account. (Imagine if you also added one of those tired old pictures of a cat hanging from a branch with two paws with the caption "Hang in there!!!") Finally, the quote, "You deserve to be good to yourself," is a very nice thought, but I recommend keeping even sweet aphorisms out of business emails.

Here's another email I'd like you to (try to) read. Get ready. This one's a long one:

From:	Egotistical Edgar
To:	Really important people
Cc:	People who aren't important
Subject:	RE: Proposal

The worthiness of an idea is, in essence, a function of both where we coexist in a certain product or economic cycle and how valuable the concept is to the key users of said idea in a specific timeframe within that cycle, and, to a certain extent, slightly beyond. That idea will have its greatest value when the above-mentioned two factors align, and also only when the time to disseminate the idea to major stakeholders is greatly reduced, and as more ideas become available during that critical time span, said idea sadly can be feckless—a fact that can be seen within assiduous environments such as ours. Secondly, in order to be expeditious about getting our proprietary techniques to market, we need to leverage all capabilities available to us, to our partners (not an easy concept for the self-identified lone wolves amongst us!), and most critically to those whose well-being we purport to provide sustenance to—our clientele. Thusly, to be incentivized we ALL must focus at the highest level of and on our core competencies, which are our key competitive advantages—and remind ourselves of it daily like a mantra, if you will.

The proposed project delivers the utmost opportunity to be relevant. Yes, the financial and analytical sorts among us will only look at the bottom line, but that is truly beside the point. Our reputation is golden and must be upheld. The proposal will help us not only maintain our paramount position but also guarantee that it will pullulate us to even higher plateaux. The missioncritical missives have already been formulated by those who have proven themselves here lo these many years.

The entire team can achieve this I believe. We need not be dependent upon distracting trends that typically glow bright then fade like mysterious phenomena physicists only cogitate about. No surprise then that my support is thoroughly behind this proposal.

Are you still awake?

If you managed to get through that acrid smog of writing, you likely discovered some noxious errata—er, sorry, bad mistakes. Congratulations on realizing that this email might win the award for "Most Incomprehensible" at the Bad Communication Annual Banquet. Before we decipher the actual meaning of the email, let me answer a few common questions.

Isn't the email too long? Yes, definitely. You probably just read (or didn't read) that email on a screen or on paper, but imagine if you had to read the entire message on your phone. You'd be scrolling down for a long time, probably becoming more and more irritated.

But before we dismiss the writer completely, let's ask ourselves what makes something too long. If your manager sent you this email and asked for your opinion, you can't very well say, "Sorry, it's too long for me. Shorten it, and then we'll talk."

The problem here is that the writer (and I'm going to make the writer male so I can use just one pronoun) seems to have no clue that not everyone wants to read every word of his masterwork. When you receive this email, you have to choose to be in it for the long haul or just not read it. And given how it's written, there's no middle ground; there's no point in the email where you can say to yourself, "Aha, now I understand." Once you decide to go for it, you have to slog all the way to the end, and waste—er, spend—time reading everything. My long answer is that the email is too long.

What's the point of the email anyway? Good question. The people who remained awake from the beginning might have noticed that the writer was replying to someone whose original email's subject line was "Proposal." Since Egotistical Edgar didn't include the original "Proposal" email in his reply, we don't know whether the original email was similarly overwritten. Perhaps at that company, the number one mission statement is "We write long emails to confuse and bore everyone. It's in our DNA."

Let's play the blame game for a minute and blame the original "Proposal" writer for not being specific in her (I chose a pronoun again; let's say her full name is Vague Vera) subject line. A better subject line could be more specific: "Proposal to Improve Market Position." Or, even better, if Vera wanted to flag that she needed feedback on her proposal, she could have written, "Need Feedback on Market Gain Proposal." Right away the readers get the context and an action step.

Edgar's job then would be to give his feedback on Vera's proposal—pretty simple action step.

When we go back to Edgar's email, we have no idea at the outset whether he's presenting an alternative proposal, agreeing with Vera's suggestion, or writing a recommendation to make him king (an idea that came from his mom). If you made it to the very last sentence, you would have seen that his "support is thoroughly behind this proposal." In other words, "I like it."

If Edgar were truly thinking about his readers and their different time sensitivities, he could have made everyone's life easier by simply changing the first sentence to "I support Vera's proposal." If that were right up front, the people who don't have much say in the outcome (i.e., the people cc'd) could decide whether they wanted to read more. Others might read on to find out why.

What's with that first paragraph, anyway? I was wondering the same thing. Since most of us are crunched for time, we appreciate when writers get to the point. That email's first sentence is a total time stopper. I bet you had to read it at least twice to understand what it means and figure out what it refers to. (I'm just amazed that he could write a sentence that is both stupefying and wretched.)

I think people write long, horrible introductions like this because they think they have a gift for writing clear and witty messages on the fly, feel they need to share their great wisdom with and inspire whoever will listen to them, or got way too much love from their parents, who told them everything they did was perfect and all of those kids who made fun of them were just jealous of their overall genius and amazing ability to write.

If I were Edgar's communication coach, I'd tell him to scratch that first paragraph (he can save it for his mom to read) and replace it with a message that most people can understand easily. Something like "I agree with Vera that our goal this year is to build on our already strong competitive position, which is based on our stellar products and our superb and dedicated workforce."

Shouldn't there be bullet points?

- Sometimes
- Because
- Bullets
- Are
- Easier
- To
- Read
- Than
- Long
- Dense
- Paragraphs

Isn't there some bad grammar? You bet. Without going into tons of detail (we'll go there later in the grammar section), here are some of the grammatical issues:

- Run-on sentences
- Bad punctuation
- Passive voice
- "Secondly" when there was no "firstly"
- Words that no one ever uses in regular speech
- Words that should be hyphenated
- Words that should be split in two
- Words that aren't really words
- Sentences that make absolutely no sense
- Zero structure

You may have noticed even more annoyances and errors. But you should be happy with yourself if you noticed any of these problems or realized that the email was basically a bunch of words tossed together to produce a rotten email salad.

Let's now figure out how never, ever to write emails like that.

Think Before You Write

In the time before we wrote emails quickly on our phones, I'd encourage people to prepare a bit before they typed anything. I still think planning is very important for the clarity of a message, but my advice now is more "Think for a second before you hit Send" rather than "Get a flip chart and map out how you should say, 'Yes, I can make the meeting.'"

The One Email Rule

I generally live by three rules: 1) the rules set by the government, 2) the Golden Rule—"Do unto others as you would have them do unto you," and 3) the rules of standard English grammar. There's also my One Email Rule: Don't write an email where the response is going to be "Why?" "Why not?" or "Huh?" In other words, get your facts and arguments straight the first time.

Here's an email that violates my One Email Rule:

> Hi Team,
>
> I'm thinking we should schedule another meeting soon.
>
> Best,
>
> Lon

This email seems simple enough. And the guy is only asking for another meeting. But think of the replies that will follow.

- "Why?"
- "When?"
- "Who should be there?"

- "I disagree."
- "I'll be traveling all next month."
- "I hate you, Lon."

See how unfair it was of Lon to write a foolish email like that? Foolish Lon. He will learn better if he reads on.

Planning Cheat Sheet

The four questions below can be considered a cheat sheet for how to plan quickly and write easily. I'll go into detail below.

1. Who's the audience?
2. Why am I writing?
3. What do I want?
4. What more do I need?

1. Who's the Audience?

Messages have to be clear for your different audiences because not everyone will understand or appreciate certain levels of detail, jargon, formality, and style. Messages can change with audiences who are, for example:

- Technical people
- High-level people
- Administrative people
- Clients
- Old folks
- Very old folks
- Young folks
- People who use numbers to make decisions

- People who use emotions to make decisions
- Time-sensitive people
- Cynical people
- People from different cultures
- People who have so much time that they sit beside their inboxes, anticipating the challenge that every ping gives them
- Some or all of the above

At times, you should also be aware of your audiences' audiences. If your job is to persuade a group of financial advisers to sell your financial product to a group of retired schoolteachers, you should think about what the schoolteachers need to hear more than what you and your fellow financially focused advisers like to talk about.

Think about how much time people will devote to reading your email. Let's quickly review the attention-span chart I covered in the section on analyzing your audience.

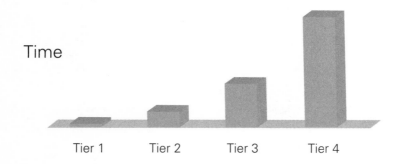

Tier 1 people have the shortest attention span and will likely only read a subject line. A subject line like Vera's above ("Proposal") would be very frustrating to a Tier 1 reader because she didn't use the subject line to say something substantive (even in four words).

Tier 2 people will read the subject line and the first sentence or two.

Review how we fixed Edgar's first sentence to something that is substantive and clear.

Tier 3 people will scroll down and appreciate good structure like bullet points to make concepts easier to grasp.

Tier 4 people will read everything, including attachments.

Tier 10 people will read disclaimers. (And people in Legal and Compliance often do.)

As a business writer, you should be prepared to write for people who might be Tier 1 or 2 so they can get the gist of your message:

> I have prepared an analysis demonstrating that we can reduce our distribution costs by 20 percent by consolidating our facilities in Denver and Kansas City to a new low-cost facility near the Salt Lake City airport.

To satisfy the Tier 4 readers, you might include this statement:

> The attached spreadsheet outlines in detail the five main steps and considerations.

Email Tone

When you're speaking to someone face-to-face, your words and the other person's words are enhanced by vocal tone, facial expression, body language, and gestures. For example, if someone at work said to you with a smile, wink, or exaggerated theatrics, "I want to scream, 'You idiots!' to those jerks who work at Reception!" you would know the person is merely frustrated and not apt to scurry down the stairs and start a riot. But if you read an email saying, "I want to severely harm the jerks at Reception," you might consider calling security, the police, or at least the people in Reception to tell them to be on the lookout.

Similarly, you could receive an email like this:

> That deadline is impossible. You're obviously not aware
> we're busy with other priorities today. Sorry.

This could make you feel like saying, "What should I do now?" The writer's underlying message seems to be "Leave me alone forever. Everything I have to do is more important than your insignificant and unimportant request, you twit."

And while the writer might be a decent person, the words "impossible," "obviously," "other," and "sorry," which may (or may not) have been chosen for effect, come across as petty, condescending, and completely unhelpful. If the writer had instead written, "We are eager to help out, but our team is in a client meeting until 3 PM today. Can one of us get back to you within the hour to discuss?" you'd feel as though the writer will do whatever she can to help you out. What a difference a few words make.

I once received an email that began like this:

> SUBJECT: . . . and?????
>
> So it seems like most people agreed with me (others didn't
> even respond). NOW . . . what do you want me to do? We
> need to move forward ASAP, everyone!

I did what I think most people would do if they received a forceful and demanding email like that: I closed my laptop, thought *Asshole*, and took a nap to reduce my panic and stress level. But consider the email's tone:

- It's unspecific—"agreed with me" on what?
- It's rude—"others didn't even respond."
- It's disrespectful—"what do you want me to do?"
- It's demanding—"We need to move forward ASAP."

The email's tone has the danger of evoking stress, resentment, or other bad feelings, which doesn't lead to a good and professional working relationship or productive results. (See above for what I did after reading it.)

On the other end of the tone spectrum, some writers are overly apologetic, resulting in extra words that dilute the main point of their message:

> I recognize that you are probably very busy right now; however, I just need to ask you if it's OK, or might be at all possible on behalf of a really important internal client, to perhaps have our project done this week instead of next?

The simple request is tempered by so many apologies ("recognize that you are probably very busy," "just need to ask," "if it's OK," "might be at all possible," "perhaps") that the writer will never get what he wants because people can easily say, "You're right, I am busy; buzz off." Here's a better version:

> High-flying internal client just asked whether we could complete the Grovel project by this Friday at 3 PM UK time. Can we set up a call today at 4 PM UK time to discuss what additional resources we'll need to complete the project by the deadline? Many thanks.

Here are my guidelines about email tone:

- Always be polite.
- Always be willing to help find a solution or propose one.
- Always be specific about what you want.
- Don't apologize for living.
- Do what the nicest, most loving grandmother would tell you to do if she saw your nasty tone.

. . . .

Should I Speak, Write, Text, or IM?

Though you may feel most comfortable communicating over text, there are times when a face-to-face chat or a phone call may be more appropriate. Here's a table to help you decide which mode is best for your content.

Speaking	· When information has any emotional component · When talking about others only in a neutral way · When you need to make a group decision · When you're trying to get to know someone better
Text	· Noncritical fast responses like "I'm on my way" · Nonbusiness-related issues that don't need to be archived or examined by Legal or Compliance, like "Made a reservation for noon"
IM/Slack or equivalent	· Quick running commentary · Quick requests

. . . .

Now that you have thought about the level of detail and appropriate tone of your email, the next step is to be clear about why you're writing and what you want.

2. Why Am I Writing?

We generally write to:

· Respond to a question

· Inform

· Request something

· Provide an update

- Give input
- Any combination of the above

You can help your readers by giving them a bit of context. Big pet peeves among people who receive more than 100 emails a day are when people write the following perhaps days or weeks after an original email was sent or an event occurred: "Yes" or "Agree" or "Did anyone ask Rik?" or "Not sure I understand" or "Please fill out the attached by Wednesday."

In each case, there's no context. Busy readers either have to scroll down the email chain to remind themselves of the background, or, if they read my book, they will email back, "You violated the One Email Rule. Penalty forthcoming. Do not move."

Better "Why" statements might be:

- Yes, I agree with Hari that marketing recycled toothpaste would not be a good strategic move.
- To prepare for tomorrow's meeting . . .
- Thanks for your email.
- Has anyone gotten back to Rik about the mysterious green leak from the radioactive waste plant above his office?
- Our team has worked on all the data analytics projects for Skiv, Flup, and Gridge over the past five years.
- We met at the Frozen Meat Scraps Convention last month.
- I am concerned that the trend of fee renegotiation will continue throughout the year.
- The Standards Bureau has asked Compliance to provide copies of all government contracts by 5 PM Central Time next Friday.

These statements give the readers a sense of background before the writer gets to her main message or request. Remember, you don't always need to write a "Why" statement, especially if your reader knows you well, has asked you a direct question, or the original email is so short you can see it on the screen below your answer.

"Hi Mom, You may remember me. I am your son."

This would be overkill. As would:

"Joe, You just asked me whether I'd like to have lunch with
you at 12:30 tomorrow."

Think about how much context you need to provide at the outset so the audience knows why you're writing.

3. What Do I Want?

Here's the chance to tell your really busy people what you want them to do or know about. A good message would be something like:

"I think the training makes a lot of sense for our team,
especially considering our upcoming expansion. I suggest
that we nominate Chela, Draggi, and Jiker, since they'll be
most involved in the project. What do you think?"

Or

"I recommend that we hold off on the Tuscany project until
next year. We'll have more momentum and credibility after
we launch Yocket."

Those examples were straightforward and to the point, and in each case would nicely follow an introductory "Why" statement.

But let's say you want your readers to know three things or respond to three things or want them to know two things and respond to two things. Your message could then be something like this:

"Can you please answer the three questions below?"

Or this:

> "Can you please answer the three questions below so I can move forward with the Gizmic application?"

Or even better:

> "As you know, Gizmic needs to certify our safety systems each year. Since the deadline is on March 31, can you please answer the three questions below by March 15 so I can meet the deadline?"

Another poor one:

> "Since I know you're interested, FYI . . ."

And the same one improved:

> "Our Asian partner sent us the attached document, which deals with how we should handle Litwitgit's response to our aggressive marketing tactics. Here are the main three points we should consider."

4. What More Do I Need?

As we saw with Egotistical Edgar's email, details can be dense. I'm a big fan of bullet points, numbering, and, occasionally, tables for clarity or readability. A simple and annoying email like this comes across as a splat of disorganization and disrespect:

Subject: Coffee disaster!!!

I've noticed several problems with the coffee machine. No one is filling up the water properly. I can't find the mocha and marshmallow powder that I like. Could we agree to clean up the sticky stuff mess in the back? Overall it was a mistake to buy this system. Who's responsible for that decision?

I am completely taken aback by the rudeness of this writer. Not only is the email accusatory and violates the One Email Rule (we'd have to email back, "So what are you suggesting we do, Smarty Pants?"), but bullets would also have helped organize the issues.

A somewhat better version could be:

Subject: Let's all make the coffee area nice, OK?

I'd appreciate everyone's help in keeping the coffee machine working well because I've noticed:
1. Not everyone is following the instructions on filling the water tank.
2. Several flavored powders (particularly mocha and marshmallow) seem to be missing.
3. The back of the machine is sticky.
I'd also like to chat about replacing the entire system.

Yes, the email is clearer with enumerated points, but the writer could have made the email even better by offering solutions rather than just stating the problem:

Subject: Ideas for improving the coffee area

Because of several problems with the current coffee-maker, I will investigate and purchase a new machine. In the meantime, can we all please agree to:

1. Fill the water tank when the red light shows it's empty?
2. Return flavor packs to the appropriate drawer and let Jakk know when you've used the last pack?
3. Clean around the back of the machine with a sponge when you fill the water tank?

Why was the last email the best example? Because the writer stayed away from emotions and playing the blame game, didn't open the problem up for everyone to offer solutions, and stayed with facts and a proposed solution to the problem. Here's how the writer might have used my planning cheat sheet to get to this better email:

1. **Who's the audience?** My coworkers, who all should technically help out, but if I sound too demanding or nasty no one will follow through. I have to make sure I don't blame anyone. What's the point of that?

2. **Why am I writing?** Several problems exist with the current coffeemaker and the messy area around it.

3. **What do I want?** I want everyone to help out. Also, maybe we should get a new coffeemaker, but I should assign someone to research it or, better, say that I'll take on that task.

4. **What more do I need?** A bulleted list with solutions rather than just problems.

The planning cheat sheet may be overkill for a quick email or a response to a simple question, but the more you keep in mind the first three steps—who's my audience, why am I writing, and what do I want—the easier it will be for you to construct emails that get right to the point. Now we're going to take this basic template and expand on it for longer emails and longer documents.

Thinking versus Communicating

The mind works this way:

Thought 1: I am hungry.

Thought 2: There's no food in my house.

Thought 3: The grocery store will be closed tomorrow.

Therefore,
Conclusion: I better go to the store now.

We much prefer to receive information this way:

Conclusion: I better go to the store now.
Because . . .

Thought 1: I am hungry.

Thought 2: There's no food in my house.

Thought 3: The grocery store will be closed tomorrow.

As you plan to communicate to most audiences, try to invert your thought process so your main message or conclusion is at the top of your email or document. Readers also appreciate seeing conclusions of each of your supporting points before you get into the supporting points' details.

Previews Help Readers Know What to Expect

I also suggest adding a preview, a brief section after your conclusive main message that orders your details and can act like a road map or table of contents for the rest of the document.

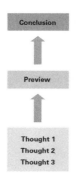

Main Conclusion, bottom-line message, or request.

Preview: Like a table of contents or road map.

Thought 1's Conclusion sentence in bold.
Followed by more details about Thought 1.

Thought 2's Conclusion sentence in bold.
Followed by more details about Thought 2.

Thought 3's Conclusion sentence in bold.
Followed by more details about Thought 3.

Example: You have to present to Ghil, Sasi, and Brig from the marketing team your initial research findings about which chewing gum high school students prefer, how your new DentystNME gum is doing in the very competitive super-sugar, cavity-causing gum submarket, and where you think the Marketing Department should focus.

1. **Who's the audience?** The very analytical Marketing Department will definitely want lots of data, but it will also want a summary and recommendation based on all my surveys and spreadsheets.

2. **Why am I writing?** The Marketing Department needs to know how to position the brand based on consumer data I compiled.

3. **What do I want?** I want to recommend that our brand, which has strong market acceptance, could increase its position by touting the extra sugar we provide per stick of gum, currently 50 grams per stick, which is currently the industry leader. Students are buying gum today based on the highest sugar content.

4. **What more do I need?** There are three main support points to show: 1) Students buy gum today because they believe the sugar keeps them awake and focused; 2) They gravitate to the industry leader—EnamylKyllyr—because they erroneously think it has the highest sugar content; 3) They like our flavors best, which is why we've seen recent brand growth.

SUBJECT: Survey: top sugar content is key for DentystNME

Hi Ghil, Sasi, and Brig,

I recently completed a ten-city, 50-high-school tour to assess how your team can best position DentystNME in the very competitive super-sugar gum market. Based on my research (see attached), I conclude that we can increase the share of our brand by emphasizing our industry-high sugar content, which is students' number one consideration when purchasing gum.

Here is what I found. (You are welcome to read more detail in my attached survey questions, results compilations, and data analysis.)

- **Students not only like extra sugar; they also crave it. More detail.**
- **Students on social media compete on how much sugar they consume daily. We have more sugar than the competition. More detail.**
- **Multiple multicolor dental fillings are new status symbol. More detail.**
- **Our flavors win in all surveys. More detail.**

Use a Good Close to Wrap Things Up

The previous email outlines the competitive advantages in specific bullet points quite well. But the writer can't just end the email after that last bullet point; there needs to be something additional to talk about what happens next.

Here are some ways to finish up that email:

· I have a meeting scheduled on Monday afternoon with the director of marketing, and I will contact you on Tuesday to discuss next steps.

· Please feel free to contact me if you have any questions.

· Remember to vote for my son, Chipper, for best T-ball player this year!

I said those were some ways to finish the email; I didn't say they were all good ways.

Reply-All Hell

Dear Someone Else's Dad,

I hate being picky, but one of my colleagues ends all her emails with the phrase "What are your thoughts?" Sometimes the request is reasonable, like when she comes up with a very specific idea and wants feedback from the team. But most of the time, I feel burdened by this request. Does *everyone* always have to give her feedback on everything? This inevitably leads to a scenario in which our 20-member team sends their thoughts in a Reply-All email, resulting in email after email of things like "Nope," "Looks good," "No," "Thanks," "Points 1–3 good; point 4 not sure," etc. It feels like a total waste of time, and the number of incoming emails this generates is annoying. Do you have any ideas on how to get her to stop?

Thanks,
Email Hater

Dear EH,

It sounds like your colleague has decent intentions but doesn't realize how she's coming across. Here are my thoughts:

1. If you know her very well and you are at the same level, you could tactfully tell her about ways the team can be more efficient over email to avoid so many Reply Alls. Maybe suggest that all of you try to ask specific people in emails for feedback (e.g., "Dag and Ulli—would love to get your comments since you already met with the client"), or simply end emails with "Please let me know if you need more info or want to discuss."

2. You can give the same advice to the entire team without singling her out with the focus on the Reply All inbox clutter. Just make sure that you don't end your email with "What are your thoughts?"

3. Pick your battles and don't let "What are your thoughts?" bother you. Yes, it sounds a bit annoying, but there are more urgent things in life to be concerned about.

Writing Longer Reports

Senior managers who write white papers or opinion pieces for their company's websites often complain that no one reads them. I feel sorry for the writers because they work very hard putting forth what often is an important industry insight.

The reality is that long pieces are daunting. Imagine clicking through a website and finally arriving at the equivalent of a ten-page paper. It's not that the topic isn't interesting; it's that it will take time to get through every word.

You may one day be required to produce a longer piece of writing. The key to writing long-form pieces is making them accessible, which means dealing with the fact that readers are not to arrive at your paper and think, "Oh goody! I finally have something long and dense to read today!" Here's how to start:

1. **Have a great title that's conclusive rather than descriptive.** A title like "Trends in Socks" may not entice me to keep reading. However, titles that contain a verb and are conclusive help your audience know the point of view. For example, "Four Ways to Extend the Life of Your Socks," "New Wicking Material Strengthens Socks, Cools Feet," "Executives Trade Black Socks for Polka Dots," or "Young Workers Shun Socks, Prefer Blisters" might make me take a look.

2. **Have an executive summary.** Remember that some people may not have time to read a long piece and may just want to quickly know the four ways to extend the life of socks. It's not a bad idea to put a box around an executive summary and use a few bullet points to make it stand out and be easy to read. Another idea is to have an abstract, or two-sentence conclusion, followed by an executive summary, which could contain perhaps five bullet-point details.

3. **Put in a table of contents.** Remember how a preview helped in emails? A table of contents creates a road map for the long document and allows readers to choose where they want to go, especially if it includes hyperlinks. I might decide that I only want to read about socks with novelty patterns and nothing about high-tech, moisture-wicking socks.

4. **Use conclusive subtitles and put them in bold.** Again, you'll allow readers to scan more if your sections begin with "Sweat socks last longer when they're washed inside out" rather than "Sweat socks issues."

5. **Consider margin notes.** To add even more accessibility in a very long document, write very short summaries—maybe just one

sentence—of certain long sessions to make readers feel that they don't have to read everything.

6. **Use a lot of simple graphs and tables.** Make sure that the graphs you use enhance the message and don't overcomplicate things. Data is great, but think about what's truly necessary to make your point. Also, give your graphs a conclusive title rather than a descriptive one: "Dress Socks Color Trends" is not as effective as "Patterned Sock Sales Surged 20 Percent Last Year."

7. **Don't save everything for the conclusion.** It's great to wrap up, but make sure that anything you put in the conclusion has been already covered in the executive summary.

Here's a good general template for how long reports can be put together:

Conclusive Title

Abstract: Two-sentence summary

Executive Summary:

· About five bullets

· ...

> Summary notes in the margins can help readers get a quick understanding of long passages

Table of Contents

Introduction

Background

Conclusive Headings All the Way Through

· Conclusive subheadings all the way through

· Conclusive graph and table titles

Next Steps

Conclusion, which should match the executive summary

The template above demonstrates that even an article about something as potentially boring as sock trends can grab different readers' interest if you structure your piece with a fickle audience in mind. Your goal as a writer in business is to make sure people take away what they need, not to make sure they read every word you write.

Don't You Want to Read 300 Pages?

Dear Someone Else's Dad,

I've taken some of your seminars and know that you always tell people to front-load messages. I've been writing some longer reports for our team, and I feel that if I write the conclusion up front, no one will want to read the rest of my work.

Thanks,

Longform Writer

Dear LW,

My message up front: It's not about you; it's about your audience. I know you've worked hard, but your audiences will appreciate you more if they have a chance to get your main point and then decide if they want to read more detail.

Basic English Grammar

You might be intimidated about writing effectively at work, particularly if you've never been confident with English grammar or your high school teachers told you you'd be an utter failure in everything except welding. You also may not be confident about grammar if English is not your first language. And since grammar is not taught to native speakers as much as it used to be, I've found that many people who learned English as a second, third, or fourth language know English grammar rules better than native speakers.

A cool thing about English is that if you're not sure how to write something with perfect grammar, you can probably work around the problem by coming up with something you know is right. For example, let's say you want to write something like "Please feel free to forward this email to whoever might be interested." Then you look at the sentence and feel unsure because you don't remember whether it should be "whoever might be interested" or "whomever might be interested." But you could simply rewrite the sentence as "Please feel free to forward this email to any other team members." The meaning is pretty much the same, you're confident the grammar is correct, and no one will know that you agonized over the "whoever" or "whomever" question. (By the way, "whoever" is correct. I'll explain later.)

Although texts, tweets, and IMs encourage shortcuts in writing and proper grammatical structure, I hope you never forget the basics of English grammar. If you flub up something grammar-wise, spelling-wise, or word-wise in an email, the old-fashioned grammar nerds (like me) in your workplace may wonder whether they can trust you to write appropriate emails to clients or higher-ups who also may be grammar nerds.

I won't go into every grammar rule in this chapter; you can find dozens of highly rated ESL or grammar books and online resources that will provide answers to specific questions you might have. I will, however, highlight some basic issues that I see a lot in typical business writing and give pointers on how to correct them.

I'm going to start with the big picture, providing some helpful thinking about grammar in the workplace, and then drill down to smaller and more specific details. For instance:

- Paragraphs (keep them short!)
- Sentences (keep them simple!)
- Word choice (be precise!)
- Punctuation usage (use for clarity!)
- Grammar rules that I find people frequently mess up (read on to see my list of the big ones!)

Let's begin.

Paragraphs Should Contain One Idea

When I was in second grade, our teacher taught us her rule: Paragraphs must have four sentences. Since I was a very obedient child, that rule stayed with me until I finished college. Up until then, I never allowed myself to end a paragraph after only three sentences. I followed this rule to the extreme, worrying that the paragraph police would arrest me in the middle of the night if they found out that I'd added a fifth sentence to what I thought was an incomplete paragraph in an essay on organic flow in 19th-century European painting.

Guess what? Paragraphs don't have sentence number limits. The paragraph police are all out of work. The content (what you're saying) should dictate the form (how many sentences your paragraph contains). Keep in mind, however, that if a paragraph looks too long in a work-related piece of writing, busy businesspeople will be less inclined to want to read it.

To help you succeed in your workplace, I offer you these guidelines (notice that I didn't use the word "rules"):

1. Start each paragraph with a topic sentence, something that helps your reader know what you're going to talk about in the paragraph. Sometimes this topic sentence is also the conclusive sentence of the paragraph (even if it's worded slightly differently).

2. Each subsequent sentence in the paragraph should support the topic sentence. Here are some examples of topic sentences you might find at work:

   ◦ "Our leadership team needs to better define the corporate culture."

   ◦ "The prototype will be ready for testing on Friday."

   ◦ "The temporary shutdown will only affect employees in Control and Purchasing."

3. Topic sentences will vary greatly, depending on what you're writing about. To determine whether a sentence is a topic sentence or not, put the word "therefore" before the sentence; since "therefore" connotes conclusion, any words following "therefore" should automatically be a conclusion of the other bits of information in the given paragraph.

Sentences Should Be Simple

At the most basic level, a sentence has a noun and a verb. When there's too much other stuff in a sentence, the main point can be lost. Avoid long, drawn-out sentences. Try to keep them simple. If you've written a rambling sentence, start over by identifying the main noun and the appropriate main verb that goes with the noun. I guarantee you'll end up with one or perhaps two simpler sentences. Here's an example:

> The associates, who were just hired by Operations Management, and who were recently trained at our new training facility in California along with analysts from the technology team, all of whom have been employed for at least two years, were able to take advantage of the beautiful weather last weekend.

In this long sentence, the main noun is "associates." The main verb is "were able to take advantage of," which seems miles away from the main noun. If we start over, we would want to put that main noun, "associates," adjacent to a better, perhaps more specific, verb. In this case, we could end up with two simple sentences that make the point clearer and make it easier to read.

> The new Operations Management associates enjoyed a free weekend during their training program in California. The two-year technology analysts also participated in the training.

In business communication, always try to be clear and keep things simple to help people quickly and easily arrive at your message. If having two simple sentences gets a point across better than a longer, fancier one, you should do that.

Keep Sentences in the Active Voice. Readers appreciate the active voice because the sentences are shorter and the flow is better. In the active voice, the main noun comes before the verb. Put another way, the actor of the action is in the beginning of the sentence. Example of the active voice: "The analyst used the active voice when writing this sentence." ("The analyst" is the actor of the action "used.") The passive voice version would be "The active voice was used by the analyst when writing this sentence." That passive sentence, while actually grammatically correct, reads a bit clunky; the active voice often gets the point across more clearly and quickly.

Here are some examples:

> *Passive voice:* The report will be prepared by the auditors next month. (Sentence is unnecessarily wordy.)

> *Active voice:* The auditors will prepare the report next month. (Sentence is more direct.)

But there can be exceptions when you may want to choose the passive voice:

- If your goal is to protect a group from blame
- If the actor of the action is irrelevant or unknown
- If you want to keep your message impersonal

Here's an example of a sentence where you would want to choose the passive voice: "The recruiting event was canceled." You might purposely want to write the sentence this way because this wording protects the people who actually canceled the event. It takes the focus away from them and puts it more on what generally happened. Depending on the work situation, using the passive voice here would not only allow people to be aware of what happened with the recruiting event but may also temper potential bad feelings about the people who canceled it. (Of course, since you did not name names in this passive-voice sentence, some of the readers may call for a formal investigation as to why this event was canceled. They may hire lawyers and private investigators and contact the local media. All because the passive voice was used.)

Sentences Should Have a Positive Form and Tone. Remember how I spoke earlier in the book about the importance of being direct and polite? This same guideline applies to sentences. When writing sentences at work, try to make definite assertions without being negative or passive in tone.

The sentence "He is often not quite able to answer questions directly," for example, is wordy, not direct enough, and has the word "not," which gives the sentence an overall negative tone. But taking the same idea and writing it as "He is usually evasive and noncommittal when answering questions" makes the sentence more direct and specific.

As another example, the sentence "Our private clients receive the same level of service and dedication given to our institutional clients" has a missing main noun ("We") but also is a mixture of passive and active in tone: one group "receives" and the other "is given." But writing the same sentence as "We provide our private clients the same specialized service and dedication that we provide institutional clients" puts the main noun up front, keeps the tone active, and makes a stronger sentence.

I recommend taking extra time to craft simple and clear sentences in emails, longer reports, and speeches to help make you a more powerful and effective communicator. Your readers will be able to efficiently and effortlessly discern what you mean, which can make you come across as focused and professional.

Fixing Common Writing Errors

Put modifiers next to what they modify. When you start a sentence with a clause that refers to something, the thing you're referring to should go right after the comma.

Example:

> As an expert in the field, the sewer should be cleaned.

Here the meaning would be the *sewer* is the expert in the field. A better sentence would be:

> Based on my expertise, I believe the sewer should be cleaned.

Here's a sentence I remember from my tenth-grade grammar book:

> Walking across the campus, the library met my gaze.

In the world we inhabit, libraries have neither legs nor eyes. The major problem here is that the main (pro-)noun, "I," is nowhere to be found. If you started to write the sentence entirely over and started with "I" you'd get: I saw the library while I was walking across the campus.

Who stole my whom? Don't quote me on this, but the word *whom* will likely be gone within 100 years if not sooner. Most people aren't sure when to use it, and when you're speaking, you're most likely going to say "who" anyway, even if you know it might be wrong. The other thing some people do is make a weird sound, cough, or wipe their mouth at the end of saying the word "who," so their audiences won't know if they're actually getting it right.

But here's how to get it right. Every noun or pronoun in a sentence has to match up with a verb. The word "who" in a clause would also like to pair up with any available verbs once the nouns and pronouns have paired up with other verbs. If there's a free verb left, "who" can grab it and go to the party. If "who" can't find any available verbs, it must turn itself into "whom."

Example:

The people who came from Mars had funny accents.

Let's match up nouns and verbs. "People" goes with "had." That was pretty easy since the basic sentence is "The people had funny accents." The clause that contains "who" has the only verb left in the sentence: "came." "Who" happily pairs up with "came," and the sentence is correct as written.

Here's another example:

The people who Johann met came from Zanzibar.

Again, let's match up nouns and verbs. "People" goes with "came," since the basic sentence is "The people came from Zanzibar." Inside the clause that contains "who," "Johann" can match up with "met." The word "who" searches for available verbs, but alas, there are none left. "Who" has to become "whom."

The correct sentence then is this:

The people whom Johann met came from Zanzibar.

Maintain parallel construction in sentences and lists. Power-Point has made life easy for people preparing presentations because of its automatic prompts that help you fill in bullet points. I wish PowerPoint would have a warning bubble saying, "Don't forget that your bullets should be grammatically parallel!" I can only dream.

Look at this slide:

Necessary procedures if your upgrade isn't working properly:

· Call the help desk.

· Having your login ID when you call will speed things up.

· Your manager should be informed of any problems.

· Sending an email to IT would be a good idea too.

· I will let you know when the upgrade is completed!

In my dream world, a balloon would pop up and say, "OK, you've got five bullet points in four different grammatical constructions. Would you like me to help make them grammatically parallel for you?" You can click "Yes Please!" or "No Thanks, I'll Keep It in the Stupid Way I Wrote It."

For argument's sake, you click "Yes Please!" The slide now reads:

The software upgrade will start automatically on Saturday local time 01:00 AM. The upgrade should not affect your ability to work. If you do get an error message on your screen, please:

· Call the help desk (x3487) with your login ID.

· Email your manager and IT about the program to keep them informed.

· Please be patient. We are committed to making the process as seamless as possible.

Each bullet point now starts with the same part of speech—in this case an active verb. Whatever part of speech you choose—verbs, -ing words, full sentences—keep all bullets in the same format.

Avoid nominalizations. Nominalizations are just noun forms of verbs. Here's a list of verbs and their corresponding nouns:

VERB	NOUN
discover	discovery
move	movement or motion
resist	resistance
react	reaction
impede	impediment
fail	failure
refuse	refusal

In business communication, sentences are clearer (and less stodgy in my view) if you use the verb form instead of the noun form. For example, "Our intention is to audit the records of the program." is stodgier than "We intend to audit the records of the program." And "It is our belief that there should be consultation by the CEO with the workers before changes to the rules are made." is much more complex than "We believe the CEO should consult with the workers before changing the rules."

Put apostrophes in the right place. Apostrophes are used to make nouns possessive and substitute for a letter in a contraction. Apostrophes are not used to make words plural. Let's use them correctly.

Let's start with this example: "My friend Sal Smith has invited me over. I am going to Sal Smith's house." Simple. If that rule works for Sal Smith, it also has to work for Pat Jones: "My friend Pat Jones has invited me over. I am going to Pat Jones's house." Yes, that is correct. But now, let's say Sal's parents have invited me over: "I am going to the Smiths' house." And if that rule works for the Smiths, it also has to work for the Joneses (yes, that's also correct—since "Jones" ends in an "s," the plural requires "es"): "I am going to the Joneses' house." Yes, that is correct. And that concludes my story about visiting the Smiths and Joneses.

Use commas appropriately based on where you live. If you were educated in a rigid, old-fashioned American elementary school, you were likely taught to use the Oxford comma, also called the serial comma. The Oxford comma is the comma before the "and" or "or" in a series of words: "We played baseball, basketball, and tennis." (Note the comma before the "and.") If you were educated in a rigid, old-fashioned British grammar school, you were likely taught *not* to use the Oxford comma: "We played cricket, rugby and lawn tennis." Today there are online groups that passionately want either to preserve or ban forever the Oxford comma. I don't want to take a stand. For me, it's all about clarity and consistency.

Here's a sentence where the Oxford comma helps clarify the meaning: "I love solid blue, solid red, or yellow-and-green-striped wallpaper." I think the comma before the "or" is a good idea to keep the three options distinct.

Similarly, I would use an "Oxford semicolon" (if something like that actually exists) to separate items in a series that have commas in them: "We visited Schmedeswurtherwesterdeich, Germany; Kvernbergsundsø-degården, Norway; and Venkatanarasimharajuvaripeta, India." There, that now seems clearer.

As for consistency, if you choose to use the Oxford comma because your company's style sheet mandates its use or because you just like it, make sure that you consistently use it throughout a document. Conversely, if you follow the AP style guide, you should be consistent in *not* using the Oxford comma.

Commas in dates can also be problematic in international communication. In the US, we write July 8, 2019 and July 2019. In most of the rest of the world, the equivalent would be 8 July 2019 and July 2019. Of course, those differences aren't too hard to decipher, but things can get confusing if you use shortcuts.

For example, 7/8/19 is read as July 8, 2019 in the US, whereas in most of the rest of the world, it is read as the 7th of August 2019. I'd avoid using the 7/8/19 date format entirely.

Quotes are also punctuated differently in different locations. In the US, a quotation mark goes after a period (what the British call "full stop") or comma, even though it might not make logical sense: "I am a big fan of the episode 'She Ate All My Tacos.'" The name of the episode "She Ate All My Tacos" doesn't have that actual period in the title, but in the US we put the quotation mark outside the final punctuation. In the US, we also start with a double quote and embed a quoted name with a single quote. In the UK, it's just the opposite: they start with a single quote and embed a quoted name with a double quote.

So the UK version would be: 'I am a big fan of the episode "She Ate All My Tacos.".' Note: if the episode's title was "She Ate All My Tacos!" you would write, "I am a big fan of the episode 'She Ate All My Tacos!'" (US) or 'I am a big fan of the episode "She Ate All My Tacos!"' (UK). In other words, you don't need a period (full stop) after an exclamation point.

Parenthetical material is punctuated the same way around the world. A sentence within parentheses is punctuated normally with the period inside the parentheses. If the parenthetical material is a fragment or clause, the final period goes outside the parentheses. It's the difference between "We had a magnificent time at the amusement park. (Sal vomited only once.)" and "We had a magnificent time at the amusement park (in spite of Sal's vomiting)."

Confusing Words

People often confuse or misuse certain pairs of words. Spellcheck won't catch the wrong usage, so it's a good idea to memorize the differences. Of course, if you still can't remember which one to use, check online to determine the meaning of the word you chose or use a synonym that means what you want to say. I've also put together a list of words that can lead you down a rabbit hole of grammar problems and words that have a different meaning in different places.

Here's a select group of words that people often confuse.

adverse/averse	*Adverse* means harmful. *Averse* means having a strong dislike. "He was not averse to driving to work, in spite of the frequently adverse driving conditions."
affect/effect	*Affect* is mostly used as a verb and means to have an influence on. *Effect* is a noun meaning a consequence or result. "His outbursts affect my ability to concentrate, but the tranquilizer I took had a positive effect on my mood." (*Effect* can be used as a verb meaning to cause to occur. "The manager hoped to effect change with her new performance plan." *Affect* is also used as a noun when psychologists refer to a patient's mood or expression. "She showed a flat affect when we spoke.")
appraise/apprise	*Appraise* means to assess or value. *Apprise* means to keep informed. "Please keep me apprised after you appraise the property."
beside/besides	*Beside* means to be situated next to. *Besides* is an adverb meaning also. "When he sat beside me, I noticed his mismatched socks. Besides, he wasn't wearing shoes."
capital/capitol	*Capital* has three main meanings: as a noun and adjective referring to money, as a noun referring to a top of a column, and as a noun meaning the city or town that is the seat of government. *Capitol* refers to the seat of government's building. "The invested capital was used to fund the beautiful capitals atop the columns of the capitol in the capital."
complement/ compliment	*Complement* means to match with (as a verb) and a match (as a noun). *Compliment* means to praise (verb) and praise (noun). "I complimented him because his brown socks perfectly complemented his brown tie."
discreet/discrete	*Discreet* means secret. *Discrete* means distinctive and unique.
farther/further	*Farther* refers to longer distance. *Further* refers to greater extent. "Let's not discuss this topic further. The pig farm is farther away than the swamp."
fewer/less	*Fewer* is used for countable items. *Less* is for noncountable items (e.g., fewer cookies versus less milk).
greater number of/ more than	*Greater number of* is used for countable items. *More than* is for noncountable items (e.g., a greater number of cookies versus more than enough milk).

i.e./e.g.	*i.e.* is Latin for *id est,* which roughly translates to "in other words." *E.g.* is Latin for *exempli gratia,* which translates to "for example." Both *i.e.* and *e.g.* are always followed by commas.
its/it's	*Its* is the possessive form of "it." *It's* is a contraction of "it is" or "it has." "It's been a long time since that alligator had its last meal. It's scary to think about."
lay/lie	You *lay* something down, whereas you yourself *lie* down. I correct practitioners who say, "Please lay down" to say the correct "Please lie down." Some people thank me; others look at me funny.
principal/principle	*Principal* has several meanings. As a noun it's used as head of a school or of a company, or when referring to money, as in what's left to pay in your mortgage. As an adjective *principal* is used to mean the main or primary item. *Principle* is a noun and means basic truth or fundamental theory or assumption.
regard/regards	Though *regard* can be used as a verb meaning consider or view, as a noun *regard* means esteem or respect, and can be used in the form of "in regard to," meaning referring to. *Regards* is used to give good wishes as in "Best regards," or "Give my regards to your family."
who's/whose	*Who's* is a contraction of "who is" or "who has." *Whose* is a possessive of a specific person. "Whose piece of cheese is this?" "Who's going to eat this cheese?" "Who's been eating my cheese?"

And here are some words that are commonly used incorrectly.

being	Phrases like "Being that it is a difficult task . . ." are too wordy. There's nothing wrong with starting a sentence with "because." Also, I'd recommend conjugating the verb "to be" instead of ever using "being." Example: "He had a hard time in the operating room, being new to surgery" is clunkier than "He had a hard time in the operating room because he was new to surgery."
incent	Yeah, yeah, people use the word *incent*, but I look at it as a lazy, shortened version of *incentivize*, which in turn was originally a lazy, shortened version of "give an incentive," which I actually prefer.

liaise	*Liaise* is used frequently in the UK to mean meet and work together. In the US, the term has a bit of a risqué tone. An American seeing "Let's liaise tomorrow" in an email might assume the writer's intentions were not honorable. The presumed next line would be something on the order of "I got us a hotel room." The British writer of the email was just looking to set up a meeting in the office.
myself	The word *myself* is fine when used properly, as in "Daddy, I did it all by myself" or "I often ask myself why the sky isn't green." Problems arise when myself is used in place of "me" or "I." When I see *myself* as a "me" or "I" substitute, I'm convinced the person didn't know which was the correct word to use so they used *myself* because it seemed to work OK. Quick reminder: "I" goes before verbs and "me" goes after verbs and prepositions. Examples that are correct: • Jai and I went to the movies. • The movie influenced me. • If you want to know more, ask Jai or me. • The argument about the movie was just between Jai and me.
table	The verb *to table*, used in American meetings, means to put the topic aside for later discussion. In a UK meeting, *to table* means to put it on the table to discuss next. This could be the makings of a good comedy sketch, if only the audience absolutely understood the difference. On second thought, forget it.

Avoiding Business Jargon, Buzzwords, and Clichés

I love hearing from young workers who ask me to translate bizarre phrases they've heard others use at work:

· "Boil the ocean"

- "Take a bio break"
- "Action this"

Welcome to the world of business jargon, buzzwords, and clichés. Just when you thought you knew English well, here comes a completely new language. And by the way, since business jargon, buzzwords, and clichés are all pretty much the same thing—phrases or words that are totally made up, used commonly in your company and nowhere else, or used by a leader in your group whom everyone wants to emulate—I'm just going to use the word "clichés" to describe them all.

Also, every company has unique acronyms ("I work in FBD in the CHQ for the GMT, which now reports to EXO with a dotted line to GIT. Currently on the Div-F Project."), which you should get to know and use appropriately as long as you are positive that the people you speak or write to understand every one of those acronyms.

Why do people use company-specific clichés? Sometimes people hear a phrase so often at work that it becomes cultural. At one company I work for, everyone is trying to "move the needle," which means they want to effect measurable positive perception or change. At another company people are "playing in the same sandbox" (working together closely) with clients or colleagues.

Remember that just because everyone else says these sometimes-bizarre phrases doesn't mean you have to, unless you really feel you'll move the needle in your manager's perception of you, since you think you're now playing very well in the same sandbox.

Problems with clichés: People in an organization start using them because someone else (probably at a higher level) did first. Once it seems that everyone drank the Kool-Aid (see below), people forget how to speak and write in plain old, simple English, which is always clearer and more specific. To get everyone to change their ways now is like herding cats (see below).

Remember that not everyone in the global workforce understands locally used words or clichés. At the end of the day (see below), bite the bullet (see below) and cogitate (see below) on whether to use clichés.

Messages from India

I do a lot of work with people from India, many of whom use the phrase "do the needful," which means *do what has to be done* but puzzles most non-Indian English speakers. I guess people who've never heard it can figure out what the phrase means, but I always recommend that people in Indian offices not use it when communicating internationally.

There's another local word that is, in my mind, brilliant, but no one outside of India uses it. The word is "prepone," which is the logical antonym of "postpone," and means *do in advance*. I think it's brilliant because if you think about it, why do we have a post-something when there's not a pre-something. In India, they'd say, "Prepone it to Monday," whereas the rest of us have to slog through the longer sentence, "Let's complete this earlier than we had originally scheduled, say Monday."

If you think about it, though, if we all accepted prepone (do something sooner) as a legitimate word, and since we already use postpone (do something later), the logical corollary would be that to do things on time would be to pone.

Cliché Bingo

We need an all-hands meeting so at the end of the day we'll be proactive and give pushback in a scalable way, which will empower us to go the extra mile.

Confused? It's from a song I wrote years ago called "Cliché Bingo" that was based on a game people used to play very discreetly during meetings. In that game, someone creates square grids—say a 5 x 5 grid—on several pieces of paper and then writes commonly used business clichés in each box of the grid. Each paper's grid has the clichés in different positions. During the meeting, people with the grids place an X in the box corresponding to a cliché used during the meeting. The first person to fill out a line of Xs horizontally, vertically, or diagonally is supposed to yell out, "Bingo!"

The problem is that people playing the game get too nervous to actually yell out "Bingo," so most people just giggle instead. I don't recommend playing the game or even giggling during a meeting.

I've included here a list of commonly used clichés, why they're bad, and a plain English substitute. Again, it's up to you if you want to use the cliché or the simple version. I welcome hearing from you on my website about clichés that run rampant in your organizations. But it is what it is (see below).

Cliché	Why It's Bad	Alternatives
All hands on deck	Some may miss the reference to working as a deckhand on a boat. The phrase is used to call everyone together.	I'd like to call a meeting for all members. We need the entire team to work on this project.
At the end of the day	Some might think that a project will need to be completed in a day, which might make a cynical person respond, "Rome wasn't built in a day," which in turn layers the conversation into multiple silly clichés.	When the project is done. The goal is. Ultimately.
Bio break	Are we studying biology all of a sudden?	Let's take a bathroom break. Why don't we take 10 minutes to stretch our legs?
Bite the bullet	Legend says that patients used to bite bullets during painful procedures like amputations as a form of distraction. Should work be *that* bad?	Yep, it's a tough task, but let's find ways for us to get it done.

Cliché	Why It's Bad	Alternatives
Break into silos or buckets	Even though most people have never lived on a farm, the visual seems so cool.	Sort our tasks or topics into specific categories.
Boil the ocean	A task that is literally impossible.	Let's not make this overly complicated. Don't work harder than you have to.
Change agents	Typical MBA speak.	Events or actions that will cause disruptions to an industry or company.
Circle back	Because everyone started saying it and it stuck.	Get back to me.
Close the loop	See above.	Finish the entire task.
Cogitate	Vocabulary show-off.	Think about.
Content is king	People need a reminder sometimes about what matters most. See also "culture is king."	We want to make sure we always have superior content.
Deliverables	More MBA speak.	Products, handouts, or anything tangible we need to deliver to a specific audience.
Drill down	From the oil industry where they have to dig through bedrock to find more oil.	Do more intensive analysis.
Drink the Kool-Aid	Very bad cliché that references a tragedy in 1978 where a leader of a cult forced his members to drink a poisoned punch, misidentified as Kool-Aid. Term is used in reference to herd mentality.	Do what everyone is doing.
Fast-track	Sounds very high tech.	Make this task a priority. Do this project first and quickly if possible.

Cliché	Why It's Bad	Alternatives
Game changer	For those who think "change agent" sounds too business-school-like.	See "change agent".
Get one's ducks in a row	Because someone felt that we needed a cliché to say "organize," they stole this term from hunters.	Organize.
Give 110 percent	Aside from the fact that this makes no sense in the real world, the phrase means do more than you're capable of. (See what I mean about it not making sense?)	Do your best.
Go the extra mile	Businesspeople love sports-related clichés. Similar to "Give 110 percent" in distance running or cycling.	Do your best.
Heavy lifting	Sounds intense, like doing super-hard work.	Very time-intensive and focused work.
Herding cats	Since it's very hard to herd cats, the phrase, which usually starts with "It's like," means to do something difficult.	A difficult task.
Hit the ground running	Sounds exciting and motivational, since it comes from combat, where troops jump from planes.	Immediately get to work with enthusiasm.
It is what it is	Filler phrase that people think is profound but adds nothing to conversations at all, and in many instances stops them dead.	[silence]
Keep me in the loop	People like the circle motif. See "circle back" and "close the loop."	Keep me posted. Keep me involved.

Cliché	Why It's Bad	Alternatives
Let's action that	Horrible attempt to turn the word "action" into a verb. Repeat after me: "Action is not now nor will it ever be a verb."	Let's do that. Let's make that an action item. Let's take action on that.
Limited bandwidth	Came from a pre-Wi-Fi time when people tried to incorporate tech terms into everyday business language. Many people had 14k dial-up modems that literally had limited bandwidth.	My calendar is fully booked. Our team doesn't have enough resources right now.
Low-hanging fruit	An overused cliché coming from the assumption that it's wise to go after the most easily attainable fruit. People I've met who grew up on farms have told me that the true low-hanging fruit has most likely been chewed on by vermin.	Easiest attainable objectives.
Move the needle	See that old-fashioned sound meter over there with the needle that moves when you speak louder?	Make a slight and meaningful improvement.
Open the kimono	A sexist cliché that no one should ever use.	Open the financial books of a company to divulge its inner workings.
Out of pocket	An overused, rather inane cliché. "Out of pocket" truly means that you are paying something from your own wallet or bank account. Conflicting sources try to explain why and when the meaning became "out of the office" or "unavailable."	Out of the office. Unavailable.

Cliché	Why It's Bad	Alternatives
Par for the course	Another sports reference (golf, in this case).	Typical.
Paradigm shift	MBA lingo again.	Big industry change.
Peel back the onion	The visual is actually pretty specific.	Investigate deeper by going layer by layer.
Pick your brain	The literal thought is kind of gross sounding.	Get your input or ideas on.
Ping me	Though mostly meaning "send me a text," it's an unspecific method of contacting someone. See "reach out."	Call me. Text me. Email me. Tap me on the shoulder. Send me an IM.
Push the envelope	Like "think outside the box," this means to perform a task in a nontraditional, experimental, and, one would hope, beneficial way.	Don't be limited by traditional ways of solving the problem. Think creatively.
Pushback	Nothing really wrong with it, just an overused way of saying "counter-argument."	Opposition, resistance, objections.
Reach out	Call, email, talk to me.	Call me. Text me. Email me. Tap me on the shoulder. Send me an IM.
Reswizzle	It sounds so hip.	Reorganize or restructure.
Revert	It sounds more professional and is shorter to use than the very long phrase "get back to me." Used very commonly in the UK.	Get back to me.
Run it up the flagpole	Very bad image of what someone has to do to get something approved.	Present an idea. Show what you've come up with.

Cliché	Why It's Bad	Alternatives
Synergize	To maximize efficiency by having two or more groups work as one.	Work together to maximize efficiency.
Table it	US: Put this topic aside for later. UK: Talk about this topic right now.	Know which country you're in before you use the verb "table."
Take the ball and run with it	Another sports metaphor (American football).	Take the lead on. Make this project your own and (hopefully) make it great.
Take offline	Talk about it privately later.	Talk about it privately later.
Tee it up	More sports (golf).	Start out.
Think outside the box	See "push the envelope."	Don't be limited by traditional ways of solving the problem. Think creatively.
Throw under the bus	Horrible phrase meaning to blame someone for a bad occurrence for the benefit of the rest of us.	(Avoid using phrases like this.)
Touch base	Stay in touch.	Stay in touch.
Value add	Positive information, work, or return over the average.	Additional benefit.
View from 30,000 feet	People think this is a bird's-eye view, but no bird I know can fly that high. It's what you can see from an airplane, or a big-picture view. Opposite of deep dive or granular view.	Think strategically.

Keep your sense of humor about these clichés. As you can see, some of them are pretty silly. Just know that more will pop up over time, and like now, you will have a choice about whether you want to use them.

• •

What's Wrong with Saying "A Little Bit"?

Dear Someone Else's Dad,

At my company, my bosses always use the phrase *de minimis*, which I had to look up and now know that it's Latin for a trivial or insignificant amount. Everything is "*De minimis* damage after the storm" or "*De minimis* response to our survey," etc. Just recently, a couple of guys at my level started using the phrase whenever our bosses are there. It feels as if they're just sucking up to show they're one of the good guys. Do I have to say "*de minimis*" too (which sounds *so* phony to me), or can I just say "not much," "small amount," or "virtually no change," which seem more natural?
Thanks,
A Little Bit Peeved

Dear LBP,

Yes, you can say whatever phrase is most comfortable for you. There will be *de min—*, uh, hardly any effect. No one will judge you for using plain English as long as your message is clear. I'd also advise your team to limit the use of that phrase, or any other similar ones used within your company, when corresponding with clients, customers, or people from different countries. Clichés don't travel well because not everyone will understand them.

Six

MEETINGS, CONFERENCE CALLS, AND PRESENTATIONS

We've talked about how to introduce yourself, how to be aware of your nonverbal communication, how to master small talk, and how to know your audience. Let's now go into more detail about how to speak in meetings, conference calls, and presentations. Most juniors will unlikely be asked to speak at conferences right off the bat, but many managers would like to know that their junior staff can speak on their behalf if necessary. Your speaking opportunities could include running a meeting, introducing your team and your work to a prospective client, or summarizing your findings to another team.

I'm going to give some guidelines on how to run meetings, organize and deliver a presentation, and persuade certain audiences. Yes, we'll deal with audiences again, but this time we'll get deeper into their heads. Skull saws not included.

Another Meeting?

Business consultants and corporate hacks have published a bunch of books with titles like *No More Meetings!*, *Meetings Stink!*, *Death to Meetings!*, *Time Suck!*, *Meetings Suck!*, *No More Death!*, etc. The moral of this story is that rarely do people see a meeting invite in their inbox and shout, "I, for one, cannot wait to attend!"

In most minds, meetings equal a waste of time. While you may not have any authority at first to improve how meetings at your company are run, I am going to suggest a few points that can improve efficiency.

First, I'll give you a list of my pet peeves about bad meetings, followed by ways to make me, er, your team happy. I dislike it when:

- Meetings don't start on time.
- People show up late so someone has to interrupt the meeting to recap what the latecomers missed (this can happen several times during one meeting).
- People haven't spent time reading documents or other information they could have read before the meeting started and could have given comments on before the meeting started.
- People look at their phones during meetings or have private conversations.
- People bring in smelly food when the meeting had not been announced as a lunch meeting.
- There's no agenda, and even if there is an agenda, no one keeps people on track.
- Someone spends a very long time updating everyone on a topic when he or she could have easily sent an email with bullet points beforehand.
- Meetings run longer than they were supposed to and not every point has been covered; conversely, meetings fill up the fully allotted time slot, even though you've basically covered everything in ten minutes.

- No one takes meeting minutes.
- Post-meeting action steps and deadlines are not defined.

I might come across like an old grump, which I actually may be. But I hope you see why those ten (and I could have included loud background noises when people dial in, eye rolling, and dismissive comments) demonstrate a lack of respect for people's time. So let me tackle how I think meetings should run.

Running Good Meetings

It may seem obvious that all business meetings should have an agenda, designated speakers, a time breakdown, and follow-up minutes. I see a big range, including some meetings that have none of the above. As a junior person, you may not have a chance to change your team's old (bad) habits, but think about how you might make a suggestion or two down the road, especially if you think your idea might make the meeting process most efficient.

Don't have a meeting if there's no need for it. I am a big fan of keeping teams abreast of updates, but sometimes a meeting can be easily replaced with an online group conversation or a series of emails. There is one caveat to this somewhat impersonal method, however: face-to-face meetings are better when emotional conversations are involved. Facial expression, eye contact, and vocal tone can embellish both upbeat and somber messages.

Make a specific agenda. Since meetings usually revolve around updates, decisions, short-term action steps, and long-range planning, break agenda items into those categories. To save time, prepare a pre-meeting agenda, which includes deadlines by which participants are to read and perhaps respond to specific items.

For example, if a team is tracking responses to a social media campaign, the responsible person for the update could prepare a report two days before the meeting so everyone can see trends, major respondents, and even a cost-benefit analysis. Further, if the responsible party has thought of options for next steps, he could present a series of scenarios, including their strengths and weaknesses, and even a recommended action. Circulating that report in advance would save meeting time.

The meeting agenda itself should include the purpose of each agenda item. Rather than:

- Social media
- Workers' strike

You could have:

- Social media tracking update
- What's working and what's not
- Next steps, including budget and timing
- Workers' strike—looks unlikely, but will have more info

Be realistic about how many items you can cover during your meeting. Save minor decisions for an email poll or ask people to email non-critical updates after the meeting instead of including them in the agenda. Decide whether you want to set the agenda with time limits. You can be ultra-specific, though that might be too rigid for most people:

> 9:07:45 to 9:10:34—Decide on new carpet color for reception area
>
> 9:10:35 to 9:11:36—Take a breath
>
> 9:11:37 to 9:15:04—Solve global climate issues

Or you could be more general, which probably would suit most groups:

> Approve bonuses for admin staff (23 minutes)

Teach staff how to operate a B-52 bomber (7 minutes)

Review how to clean office refrigerator (20 minutes)

Make sure the moderator truly moderates. A good moderator will make sure that:

- Participants stick to the agenda.
- Someone is taking minutes.
- Messages are paraphrased and understood by all.
- Action steps, including deadlines and responsible parties, are clear.
- Everyone gets a voice.
- Everyone gets out on time.
- The minutes are distributed shortly after the meeting and contain a clear summary of what was covered and who's responsible for next steps.

Decide on a code of ethics. OK, I don't want to live in a police state, but I find it helpful for teams to demonstrate respect for people's time. I've worked with several companies where meetings have become free-for-alls: people interrupt, shout, mutter things under their breath, storm out, gang up on coworkers, have a hair-pulling brawl, etc. (I've seen hair pulling only once.)

When I work with these dysfunctional teams, I ask them to make a list of values that all team members must sign and abide by. Examples might be:

- Agree on shared goals.
- Be prepared and show up on time.
- Respect all opinions.
- Be attentive.

I can't promise that every meeting will run without glitches if people follow my guidelines, but I think that my tips can help smooth out some typical gripes. I'm also not suggesting that you burst into your second meeting and say, "This whole meeting thing is clearly an inefficient waste of time. Have you seen what Someone Else's Dad suggested? No? Then read his book and you'll see how to run a meeting!" (Note: direct them to someoneelsesdad.com or amazon.com.)

Or just see how things go, and if opportunities arise, make an occasional suggestion to help make people's lives easier.

Do I Have to Pat the Bunny?

Dear Someone Else's Dad,

My boss hates interrupters in meetings, so she has a stuffed rabbit that we have to pass to anyone who wants to speak. No one can interrupt when someone is holding the rabbit. If you want to speak next, you have to raise your hand and wait until someone gives you the rabbit. This makes me feel like I'm in preschool, and I want to rip the stuffing out of the rabbit. Is this normal corporate behavior?

Thanks,

Reluctant Bunny Patter

Dear RBP,

I'm not sure if you're asking if having a stuffed rabbit in a conference room is normal corporate behavior or if wanting to tear the stuffing out is. In either case, there really isn't any "normal" corporate behavior anymore. If I were running the world, er, sorry, a team, I'd care most about a commitment toward shared goals and responsibility and doing it with politeness and grace. Yeah, the cynic in me understands why you think the rabbit trick is a bit childish (and also not a good role model for how to treat live rabbits), but maybe it's your boss's way of maintaining some civility.

continued

If things have been running very smoothly, I'd say just deal with the bunny passing. If you and your colleagues are collectively bothered by it (cruelty to faux animals), you could tell your boss that since you think everyone has been well trained not to interrupt, you could try a meeting without Fluffy and see how it goes.

How to Handle Yourself at Meetings

Your first time to present something at a meeting can make you nervous, particularly because people often put pressure on themselves to say the *perfect* thing. To ease into the task, you may want to ask your manager whether you can have an assigned role at an upcoming meeting, like giving some background or explaining findings. Once you become more comfortable, you can test the waters (another sports cliché, see boating, swimming) by clarifying an issue, sharing an opinion, or answering a question. And once you're comfortable doing that, you should make it a point to say at least one decent thing (not inane, like "Our offices are located on the eighth floor!") at meetings to demonstrate your value to the discussion.

Before we talk about how you can feel more comfortable speaking at meetings, read what people have told me after they were slated to speak:

- "I was super prepared, but my boss told me afterward that I gave way too much detail, so the audience got frustrated and bored."
- "I was told I was going to have thirty minutes to speak, but when I got there, they said I could only speak for five."
- "The audience started asking questions right away, so I got derailed and never got to my message."
- "I was so low energy and monotone that the audience slowly became hypnotized by my droning voice and went into a trance, so I took pictures of them and shared them on Instagram." (I never actually heard anyone say this, but that would be pretty funny. Still, if it happens to you, don't take pictures.)

Given these typical comments, here are some things to keep in mind.

Try to find out beforehand what your role will be. If you're told simply to be there to listen, take good notes. And even though it's easier to take notes on your laptop, think about using paper and a pen, because you never know whether some people will think you're watching funny dog videos. If you do take notes on your tablet or computer, you could say, "I hope you don't mind that I'll be taking notes on my laptop/tablet/phone."

Don't ever underestimate the power of the recap. Once you become more comfortable with your position on your team, you can demonstrate your value to the meeting by quickly recapping the main points of one topic along with related assigned follow-up steps before the meeting participants move on to the next point. People will appreciate that someone has been listening carefully for the main takeaways.

Remember that listening carefully during a long meeting is exhausting. Compound this personal energy expenditure with a warm room and a distended after-lunch belly, and you'll be ready for an unplanned siesta. I've seen some people's beautiful handwritten notes at the start of a meeting deteriorate to a line of incomprehensible squiggles as eyelids got heavy. Bring coffee, tea, and/or lots of water to make sure you don't become known as the meeting hibernator.

Watch your timing! If you're slated to present at a meeting, find out what your audience expects from you in terms of level of detail and timing. As you see from some of the quotes at the beginning of this section, you can annoy an audience when you overstay your welcome. If you are expected to speak for longer than five minutes, make sure you have a two-minute version and even a 30-second version just in case timing is not on your side.

Send a summary email immediately after the meeting. I always recommend that presenters send an easy-to-comprehend and not-threatening-to-look-at (meaning short) summary of what they said at the meeting. You can add supporting pages like spreadsheets to enhance some of your points, but I'd advise not sending the spreadsheet as an attachment to an email that just says, "As discussed," "As requested," or "FYI."

Meetings are a part of business life. We all get used to them, and we actually enjoy them when we walk away feeling that everyone is working together toward a common goal. If you can master meetings, you'll demonstrate yourself to be not only a solid team contributor but also a key player in your company.

Speaking on Conference Calls

It's very common to have members join a meeting virtually, either by conference call or videoconference. Similar preparation guidelines—agendas, timing, and sending in advance critical documents—should apply to conference calls and to regular meetings. Conference calls are a good way for team members in remote locations to stay involved, but participants can be at a slight disadvantage because:

- They don't see the nonverbal communication of everyone in the room, so they may not know how their comments are perceived.

- They might find it hard to get a word in when people in the room are speaking over each other or when several people are having a semi-quiet private chat.

- Their phone lines may not pick up their voices well, and they also may not hear people sitting far from the conference room microphone.

In addition, if you're in the conference room making a comment you hope a remote person dialing in will respond to, you have no idea whether he is reading his email, checking Twitter, or doing yoga. Here are some ideas to engage all participants:

- Use people's names a lot. If you want Boris, who's calling in from Toronto, to respond, say, "Boris, I'd love your comments on what I'm about to say." Boris, or anyone else you call out, will get out of downward dog position immediately and pay attention.

- Articulate well. With all the noise in a large conference room full of people, move closer to a mic and over-articulate your words in a strong voice so there's no misunderstanding.

- Include remote speakers. If you're in a position to do this, find a time during the call to make sure that remote speakers have heard what they've needed to hear and said what they've needed to say.

- Keep visitors away. If you're the one calling in remotely, keep children and pets away. ("Shep, down! No! Hush! Sorry, guys.")

- Don't eat. You can figure out why.

People enjoy videoconferences because you can add nonverbal cues to your remote meeting and avoid travel expenses or jet lag. Here are a few issues to be aware of about videoconferences:

- Be aware of time differences. Coordinating a global videoconference may force you to call in from home either very late at night or early in the morning, so find a place in your apartment or house that doesn't show too much of your personal situation. People know that you're working from home, but no one needs to see your posters of acid rock bands from the '90s. I've had the uncomfortable experience of seeing participants in their bedrooms next to unmade beds and open dresser drawers. (At least no one I've spoken with has ever been wearing pajamas.)

- Know where the camera is. Since your camera and the screen where you see other participants are in slightly different locations, try to look into the camera when you're speaking to give the impression that you're giving your audience eye contact.

Old Folks and Tech

Dear Someone Else's Dad,

I'm on an international team, and we use audio-activated video-conferencing. Our faces appear in little squares on the side of the screen, and when someone starts to speak, that person's face fills the screen's background. A couple of people always forget to turn off their phones, so each time their phones ping from an incoming text, their distracted faces fill the whole screen for a moment. It gets to be pretty funny, since the offending parties seem to be clueless about what's going on, and I have to keep myself from chuckling when I see these older people squinting their eyes at their phones. How can I tell them how funny (yet unprofessional and distracting) it is without offending them?

Thanks,

Holding It In

Dear HIL,

Since they are clearly unaware of what's happening, you should talk to the "older people" in private conversations. Also, you should use the humor in the situation to make light of the technology that the "older people" don't understand. "Older people" will be happy to know that all it takes is to turn notifications off, but you may have to walk them through it since "older people" might not know how to do it. A simpler piece of advice: at the beginning of the call, remind people to put themselves on mute—turn off their microphones—while they aren't speaking. Most old codgers know how to do that.

Giving a Presentation or Speech

A client recently asked me if a presentation begins when the speaker enters the room or steps up to the podium. (By the way, this is a forced-choice question. It's like asking if someone is a cat person or a dog person. In this question there are actually more potential answers than the questioner is forcing on you: you could be definitely a dog person, neither cat nor dog person, equally both cat and dog person, a dog, though Rottweiler-leaning person, or a mixture of alternatives such as a half-Siamese, half-Sphinx person but only in March.) My answer, by the way, to the presentation-starting question was, "It all depends." It's a lame answer, I know—sort of like "It's complicated." Both of those answers will cause the questioner to say, "Sorry, what do you mean by that, dude?" (I assume everyone calls me dude when they ask me follow-up questions.)

Preparing Your Content

Here's why it depends and why it's complicated. Successful presentations require a lot of planning. Here are some steps that can allow you to do a great job.

What Do You Want, Anyway?

It's important to define your goal before any encounter, especially when your audience's time is limited. The first question I ask people before they are about to make a speech, write an email, or attend or conduct a meeting is "What would be your absolute best outcome based on what you want your audience to do or understand?"

These are examples that answer my question well:

- "I want her to be impressed with my progress."
- "I want him to approve my budget for next year."
- "I want them to acknowledge that there are alternative solutions, and we need further research before making a decision."

- "I want them to understand how to use the new system."
- "I want them to become very familiar with the new ad campaign."

The second question I ask is "Why is that goal relevant?" I call this the "so that" question. If you add "so that" at the end of your first statement, your audience will have a better understanding of the stakes at hand.

Here are the same statements I have above with the added "so that":

- "I want her to be impressed with my progress so that she can recommend me for the promotion."
- "I want him to approve my budget for next year so that we can move forward on the initiative, which will make the audit team more efficient."
- "I want them to acknowledge that there are alternative solutions, and we need further research before making a decision so that we don't spend more money than we have to."
- "I want them to understand how to use the new system so that they can instruct their teams."
- "I want them to become very familiar with the new ad campaign so that they feel that we have the strongest product in the market."

Defining a very specific goal for what you'd like to achieve at the end of either a small sitting-down office presentation or an arena-style multimedia event can keep you on track as you think about the content you need to include. Having that defined goal will hopefully encourage you to say up front what you are recommending.

Who's the Audience?

Presentations are all about the audience. Your job is to make sure that your content is relevant to your audience and give them information that will help them achieve some of their goals. As part of your preparation, similar to how you prepared to write in chapter 5, you should answer some of these questions about the audiences you'll be presenting to.

What do they want, anyway? Even if you have many audience members with conflicting priorities, think about what they all have in common. Increasing profitability, productivity, or prestige? Finding the best and most cost-effective vendor?

How much detail do they need? Some audiences are very detail oriented, while others are bottom line focused. Just as we discussed in previous chapters, try to satisfy the needs of all audiences by hitting your main conclusion first, then going into detail where appropriate.

Who's your audience's audience? Your audiences may have to take the information you've given them and present it to another audience. Your "secondary" audience could be final decision makers who need a strong pitch to be convinced to move forward, a board of directors who want to make sure all systems are going according to plan, or individual customers who need to hear how your product will provide them with the best solution.

What stories will resonate with them? A great way to make sure a presentation is memorable and focused is to think about real-life or even hypothetical stories that relate to your main point. Your audience will be more likely to remember your presentation if they can visualize a practical application of your message.

The Beginning: A Very Good Place to Start

Here's an answer to a question I'm often asked: No, you shouldn't start off with a joke. I particularly stress this point with people who are not naturally funny. I've seen some presenters start out with something "humorous," and watch them go down a dark slide of totally unfunny embarrassment. I sit in the audience squirming and thinking, *No, please, don't go there. Stop now! Ugh. Oh man, I feel so sorry for you.*

Here's an acronym that I hope will help you start your presentation: MYRA, which stands for Me, You, Recommendation, Agenda. Here's what I mean.

Me: At the outset, you should say something to raise your credibility for a specific audience. For people who don't know you, you may have to clearly introduce your name, perhaps whom you work with, what team you're on, what project you've been assigned to. For other audiences, you may have to include something about your prior work experience or your education background.

For others—think of people you work with or see every day—introducing your name and position would seem silly. In those cases, you may want to start with what you've been working on, what relevant things you've accomplished, or what people you've spoken with since the last meeting. Your goal is for the audience members to nod appreciatively and think, *Hmm, I see why this person is speaking to me today.*

Consider these examples:

- "First, let me introduce myself. I'm Lola Bola. I work on the Kitty Krunch UK team with José and Min."

- "I'm Niki Piki. I've been a specialist in the renewable garbage sector for about ten years, most recently at Trashcow and previously at Stinkaway and Slimemold."

- "Since our last meeting, I've completed the study on the effectiveness of wooden versus metal crutches and have spent time with Nat's team to make sure our results are consistent."

You: Here's your chance to demonstrate that the content you're about to present is relevant to the crowd. It's almost like saying, "Hey, guys, I know what you're thinking about/what you care about/why you're here." Just like in the Me section, you want to deliver an appropriate message that will cause the audience to nod appreciatively and think, *Hmm, I see that this person knows what it's like to be me right now.*

At this point your audience members should be more relaxed because they will recognize that you've done some research and have made a clear link between the topic you'll be presenting and how it affects them.

Here are some examples:

- "I know from our call last week that you're exploring the idea of replacing your existing window-washing vendor because you're concerned about long-lasting stains from accidents involving low-flying birds."
- "We have all discussed in detail how much our team needs to find ways to be more efficient in disseminating information to our customers."
- "I understand that your top priority is to book higher-margin assignments this year."
- "I recognize that your time is limited, but I know you're eager to find the best partner to work with you on the rat extermination project."

There's Something about You

Very skilled presenters can use this You portion to tell a quick story that relays an experience of a client, customer, user, or employee. If properly crafted, the story can help the audience visualize a situation and empathize with the protagonist.

If, for example, you are trying to increase market share with a target audience—teenagers, for example—you can say, "Before we get deep into the presentation, I'd like to bring up a quick story of a sixteen-year-old named Skye who spends every day after school working at a Fridgy's ice cream store."

For this storytelling technique to succeed, the presenter has to be very clear about the obstacles Skye faces. Skye's situation should also be representative of those of a very large number of other teens in that particular market. At the end of the story, the audience should be sitting at the figurative edge of their seats, thinking, *Something has to be done!* Now you've got 'em.

Recommendation: Now that you've gotten your audience pleased and excited with your perfectly tailored Me and You statements, you should be looking at a sea of expectant people's heads nodding together in a beautiful 4/4 rhythm. Now you are ready to hit them with your main, conclusive, bottom-line, most comprehensive statement.

Remember the sentence you thought of when I asked what you wanted to achieve at the end of the presentation? When giving your recommendation, master the skills of being polite, specific, and direct. Saying "So give me $3 million right now, bozos, and I'll take care of it" won't cut it.

Here are examples of what I mean:

· "At the end of the presentation, I hope you'll see how my analysis of Brittleburgh's economic renaissance supports our strategy of investing in the mid- to upper-income markets."

· "I'll make sure you know how to follow the specific procedures our building management gave us on how to evacuate the premises if the dance club next door plays horrible music."

· "I recommend that our group retain Chockfulla Tech to upgrade our security systems at a cost of $4 million."

· "My goal today is to have you understand that we have achieved strong portfolio returns because we consistently follow an extraordinarily disciplined process that takes advantage of our proprietary risk analyzer and the expertise of our team members, who have invested successfully over several difficult market cycles."

Agenda: You've rocked it so far. You gave the audience a reason to stay in their seats because you told them that you understand what they care about, you've proven that you're the best person to present to them, and you've given them a clear, conclusive message. Now your audience is sitting there eager to hear some more details.

As you decide what details to include, you need to ask yourself which areas of the presentation you need to flesh out. For instance, have you said enough about:

- Why I'm speaking and why's it's important
- What the process is; what the details are
- How it will work

I recommend keeping the list of the details you'll discuss to three. People can often remember things in threes, and people also likely won't feel overwhelmed when you tell them there are three items you'd like to cover. When you're finished with the second point, they'll think, *Whew, only one more point to go, then I'm off to Disney World!*

Of course, each one of your three detail points might have several subpoints, but you'll do everyone a favor by doing your homework and grouping items into three broad categories.

Enumerated Points

Don't you hate when people say, "I have three points," and then they talk for a while and eventually say, "Which brings me to my final and most important point"? You start wondering what the first two points were, because the speaker never flagged points one and two. And as you're wondering what those first two points were, you're not paying any attention to the final and most important point, so you've missed the gist of the whole speech and you might as well have just gone to get ice cream.

My final and most important point is after you say "I've got three points," you have to say "first" or "number one." And my second most important point is make sure you say "number two" somewhere along the way, or else some rude person might yell out, "Are we gonna have to wait longer for you to get to your next point?"

After you've done your Me, You, and Recommendation, you can say things like:

- "So, what I'd like to do is touch on three things: first, go into more details of why our GumSnapper app has become the go-to waste-of-time app among all thirteen- to sixteen-year-olds; second, I'll give a demonstration on how it works; and third, I'll go through the financial considerations."

- "I'd like to talk about three topics: number one, the current problem with our systems and how it has prevented us from achieving our growth targets; number two, the options we considered; and, finally, how we recommend working."

- "Based on our conversation with other customers, I think it might make the most sense for me to talk about one: the details of our terrific performance spaces and how they can be used for many types of events; two: some examples of how we've solved problems for people like you; and three: how we can work with your budget."

I recommend that after stating a recommended agenda, presenters say something like the following: "Does that make sense?" "How does that sound?" "Before we go into those or other points, I'd like to get to know what's on your mind," or "That's what I was thinking, but I'm happy to talk about anything you'd like and in whatever order you'd like to proceed."

You don't want to appear too rigid with your agenda, but then again you want to show that you're prepared to talk about what you think is the right amount of detail. A participant might say, "In the interest of time, would you mind going right to the budget?" You could say, "Excuse me, didn't you hear me when I said what our agenda was going to be? Shut up and be patient till I get there." Then again, you could preferably say, "Sure."

. . . .

TMI

I've worked with many technical people—not just people in technology but also in fields like law, economics, and engineering—where the presentations are chock-full of more technical detail than many nontechnical audiences need. Why? Typically because most well-educated people got extra points in school when they showed their work. In business you get extra points for simplicity. There's no need to "dumb it down" for nontechnical audiences, but I always recommend that technical speakers put themselves in laypeople's shoes and think about the most basic messages and elements of support those audience members need.

. . . .

Preparing for Questions

When presenters ask me whether it's OK to say at the outset of a presentation, "Please hold all your questions until the end," I say, "Sure, if you want to show everyone that you're a control freak." If you're standing at a podium and delivering a formal presentation, you're less likely to be interrupted with questions than if you are presenting to a team at a conference table.

In that more informal conference-table setting, questions mid-presentation are fair game, so you should take that into consideration when you're preparing. Warning, however: if questions about a small point get out of hand, you'll have to take control of the proceedings. Try to get back to your message and your agenda.

If you know your audience well, you'll have a sense of the types of questions they'll ask you. After you've completed putting together your presentation, write out every conceivable question your audience may have for you and then divide them into the following three categories.

The Definites. Assume you told your audience your recommendation, stopped cold, and then said, "Any questions?" The top three or four questions they'll definitely ask will likely be so basic that you probably will be answering those questions anyway in your upcoming details. (In fact, if you wrote down what you think they would ask after hearing the recommendation alone, you'd have a pretty good outline for your whole presentation!)

The answers to the "definite" questions should already be included in your presentation, and you shouldn't wait for anyone to ask them.

The Probables. The probables are the ones your audience will likely ask to:

· Challenge some of your points

· Delve deeper into your rationale

· Ask about alternative solutions

· Discuss potential obstacles

· Figure out next steps

If time allows, you can include answers to these questions in the main part of the presentation. For the others, write down your answers to any probables and think about preparing just-in-case slides or handouts, which can make answering the questions easier.

The Unlikelies. The remaining questions on your list should be those that actually could come up but probably won't. Even though you don't have to prepare just-in-case handouts to these questions, you should think about how you would answer them.

Delivering the Presentation

Once you've put together your content, refined your visual aids, and defined which stories and anecdotes make sense for the specific audience, you should think about a few more things before your big presentation.

Get to know your surroundings and equipment. I've been in presentations where everything seemed to go awry: a projector didn't work, lights went out suddenly, a video didn't play, the room didn't free up on time, a fire alarm went off, coffee and food spilled over handouts, the teleconference's sound and video cut out, a pipe burst, horrible music played loudly in the next room, and a horse galloped in. OK, not the burst pipe. And I wasn't the presenter. In most cases.

Get to your venue early. Test all your equipment, make sure that any handouts are where they need to be, and confirm that you'll be able to have good eye contact with all audience members from where you'll be sitting or standing. You can even practice a few lines from your presentation to see how loud you'll need to be so the people in the back can hear you. If someone walks in while you're speaking loudly to an empty room, you can go into a spontaneous coughing fit, immediately take out your phone and pretend you're speaking loudly on a conference call, or just be honest and say you were practicing.

Be very aware of timing. If you are allotted 30 minutes for your presentation, try not to have more than 20 minutes of material. Leave enough time for questions. If a questioner derails you in the middle of your presentation by going off on a long tangent, be respectful. Listen carefully, answer the best you can, and ask others in the room for validation if appropriate.

Monitor the clock during your talk. Allow yourself to skip over some material to finish on time. People will complain if you go over your allotted time, but no one will ever complain if you let them go early.

PowerPoint TMI

Dear Someone Else's Dad,

When my boss delivers PowerPoint presentations on-screen in a large auditorium, he projects overly detailed, all-black text on white-background, tiny-font slides. When I tell him that no one

continued

can read any of the words, he answers that his audiences appreciate seeing all the details. Who's right?

Thanks,

I Prefer Pictures

Dear IPP,

The audience is always right. In your boss's case, I don't know why he says his audience appreciates seeing illegible type. Maybe he feels the crowd will pay more attention to him since they can't read the screen. Or maybe he knows that many of his audience members will take photos of his slides, in which case more information per slide would allow the photo snappers to take a lot of detail home with them.

If, however, the slides are truly illegible, here are three solutions (if you're in a position to persuade your boss): 1) Have two files: a presentation one with clear, large font showing basic main points—maybe five bullets per slide max, and a handout (distributed in print form at the venue and also emailed) with tons of details; 2) Add a slide that summarizes main points before each text-heavy slide; 3) Tell the audience that slides may be hard to read, so he'll clearly explain them.

Dealing with Nervousness

Most people hate speaking in public because they fear they'll be judged like a bad food truck on Yelp. Or they feel they're going to mess up somehow and then become the center picture of a never-disappearing meme that says, "Wanted: Arrest for Fraud!"

We also have physical manifestations (racing heart, sweaty palms, dry mouth) when we're nervous, and we think that everyone is going to notice and point them out to their fellow audience members, who will all giggle uncontrollably together. But I've got news for you: most of these nervous manifestations aren't really noticeable (can anyone actually see your heart racing?), and your audience is generally too busy dealing with what's on their minds to care about your nerves anyway.

Being nervous is a natural human feeling, so I'd never tell anyone, "Don't be nervous, you moron, do you think anyone cares about you? Now go out there and fail!"

Here are some tips on how to calm yourself down when you feel nerves are taking over.

Talk to some audience members before you have to present. Introduce yourself to those you don't know and give them a flavor of what you'll be speaking about, especially as your topic relates to them. Have some easy small talk with those you do know. Hopefully, this early schmoozing time will make it easier for you to transition to your more formal presentation because it will seem as though you are just continuing a conversation.

Find a quiet place to do some focused breathing. From either a sitting or standing position, inhale deeply through your nose, hold for a second or two, and then slowly exhale through your mouth. As you take in each breath, focus on relaxing areas of your body too. For example, during your first inhale, you can concentrate on clenching your feet, then releasing the tension as you exhale. Then move upward to your calves and eventually all the way up to the top of your head. This exercise is not a bad thing to do on other days too.

Review your presentation's transitions and flow. Since you'll likely know your material well, just remind yourself of the order of the slides. Trust yourself that you'll embellish each slide with a story that pops into your head.

Don't worry if you forget something. No one will know if you forget a side point, so don't stand there berating yourself that you messed up. You can always say, "Oh, one thing that I forgot to mention earlier is . . ." Or you can decide to move on.

Develop good eye contact. Look out there for some friendly faces, especially those with whom you just schmoozed. Enthusiastic nodding (not nodding off) heads will help you realize that your message is coming across well.

Have some water nearby. One nervous manifestation that has a real easy fix is a dry mouth. You can take a sip of water. It's allowed. People drink water all the time. I guarantee the people out there won't be sitting there asking one another, "Wonder why she's drinking? I bet it's nerves." They also won't shout out, "You're nervous! That's why you sipped water, not because you're thirsty! Ha, ha, ha!"

· ·

Reality Check at a Presentation

What you're thinking just before you start to speak:

- · "I'm a poster child for #loser."
- · "They're all staring at my big zit."
- · "I look fat."

What they're thinking just before you start to speak:

- · "I hope the presenter will tell me something interesting."
- · "I think I'm getting a big zit."
- · "I look fat."

· ·

I Need Drugs!

Dear Someone Else's Dad,

I get so nervous when I have to present that I feel I should pop an antianxiety pill to calm me down. Do any of your clients do that?
Thanks,

Nervous Nancy

Dear Nancy,

I have no idea whether people I work with are on any kind of medication; it's really none of my business. I am not a doctor (sorry, Mom), and I can't say whether medication can help you or not. The only lay advice I can give is that if you've never been on a drug before, you don't know what side effects could be in store for you. Maybe it's not a good idea to test something new before a high-stakes meeting.

Please remember that even though you may feel nervous, your audience won't notice. You should feel more confident in your ability to present if you spend time practicing your talk with a colleague who can give you feedback on what's clear and interesting for your audience. Also, your visual aids should act as good prompters for your spoken content, so if you run through your talk a few times beforehand, you'll get to know how your story flows.

Finally, here's a trick that seems to work for some people who say they are much calmer answering questions than delivering a speech: psych yourself out to answer the question "What would you like to talk to us about today?" Then start your speech.

Seven

TEAMWORK

Many books exist on how to form the perfect team. Some focus on mixing people with different social styles to allow team members to learn from one another's different problem-solving strategies. Others focus on bringing together people who strongly prefer to take on specific tasks. All the books purport to make teamwork more efficient.

I don't want to contradict or support any given method because I think that the success of teams is a combination of factors—most specifically, unanimous commitment, clarity of goals and tasks, and assignment of tasks to people with the appropriate skills and personality styles.

How to Put Together a Good Team

Junior people are often tasked with either putting together a team or running an existing team when a manager is busy with other matters. Here are some issues to consider.

Define specific and reasonable goals. Statements like "increase profitability" may be motivational, but they're a bit lofty and unspecific. A team needs to have reasonable goals. "Increase operating margin by 20 percent this year" may overwhelm some, but if the metric is reasonable based on your infrastructure and resources and you know that the goal is in line with your managers' expectations and overall goals, make the statement the team's mission.

Choose people with diverse strengths. When we were in school, it was fun to work in a team with our friends because we all got along, had fun while we worked, and just cared about getting a decent grade. If you were to do this at work, potential outcomes could be a daylong party, a vicious fight for control, perpetual brainstorming sessions, or people working individually. In all cases, nothing substantial would ever get done.

Instead, invite people who have demonstrated success in how they approach problems and work with others. Of course, we all want to work with people we like, but a reason to bring someone on board should not only be because she is nice. I'd vote for including someone I might not particularly like but who either has strong influence over a key group whose support would be critical or has strong skills in an area, like accounting, for example, that others don't.

Here are some more ideas when deciding whom to add to your team:

- Someone with strong organizational abilities whom you can count on to keep track of tasks and metrics
- Someone with a wide network within the firm—perhaps to the c-suite or technology team
- Someone who is also part of a related functional team that you may want to petition for resources
- Someone whose personality has helped smooth over conflicts because of their superior listening and negotiating skills

If you work in an organization that assigns people to teams rather than giving people a choice about whom to choose as team members, the team leader should make a point of learning what people's strengths are.

Get commitment on goals, metrics, and timing. You could ask everyone for a signed contract to agree on what you want to achieve or even do a bloodletting ritual, but Legal, HR, and the carpet cleaning company might object. A spoken commitment may be enough. If you've chosen the right team members, their neurons may be automatically firing in the ways you want them to. Use the time to encourage ideas, but also to flatter the strengths you know your team members have. "Gerri, your relationship with the data team was critical when you worked on the Plumper project. How do you think we can be a part of this one?"

Be a role model but not a martyr. Once you've figured out which people will work on which tasks and you've produced a project plan with specific metrics and deadlines, make sure you follow through on what's expected of you. No matter how you choose to check in for the next meeting, group call, or teleconference, make sure you and others show that your tasks are complete.

Just a warning: don't play the martyr game. Watch out for emailing things like "Lon and I seem to be the ONLY ones who worked ALL last night. I missed my daughter's final piano recital, by the way, to make sure that we finished the tasks WE ALL SAID WE WERE GOING TO COMPLETE by the deadline. Did anyone else do ANYTHING?" Oh, shut up.

Be gentle with slackers. If people aren't able to execute, don't embarrass them in front of the team. The slackers know that they're slackers and don't want to be called out. You can speak to them privately and ask if the tasks they've taken on add too much to their workload, and then ask them how they suggest you move forward. Don't keep slackers on the team if nothing improves. You have work to get done.

What I've suggested here goes in tandem with the tips I have in chapter 6 on managing meetings: the more you stick to a plan and the more you communicate clearly with your team members, the more effective and enjoyable your experience can be. I love working with my closest work friends, but they may not be the ones who'll contribute to the most successful outcome.

Make Your Group's Voice Heard

Dear Someone Else's Dad,

A manager—call him Dirk—from another division asked me to represent my division on a company-wide task force. I'm very junior and seem to be a lot younger than everyone else on the task force. I know that Dirk and my manager don't exactly see eye to eye, so I think I was chosen for the task force because I don't know a lot and won't make waves. I don't want to be a silent participant, let Dirk intimidate me, and then have him find ways to do things my manager won't like. Do you have any tips on how to handle this?

Thanks,

Quiet Quincy

Dear Quincy,

Welcome to the world of internal politics. I don't know Dirk's motives, but your assessment sounds reasonable. If he has chosen you to represent your division, you have to be clear about how every item you discuss in the task force affects your group and other groups. Look for opportunities in those meetings not to be a naysayer but to articulate pluses and minuses for everyone. Your responsibility as a member of a task force is to do what's right for the entire firm. You may get a reputation among other task force members as someone who looks at a bigger picture than Dirk does.

Eight

THE LANGUAGE OF FOOD

When you work closely with others, you'll learn their meal habits, likes, and dislikes. You'll see people bring lunches containing foods you've never heard of and that may initially disgust you; you'll see people who prefer to eat at their desks every day; and you'll see people who leave their dirty dishes in the kitchen and expect people to clean up after them. It's sort of like having a lot of roommates.

Sometimes managers may order in food for everyone from their favorite places, which pretty much everyone else hates. Don't feel you absolutely have to partake, but be gracious. I worked for a manager who loved a now-closed Chinese place called City Luck, which everyone else in our office despised and called either City Yuck or Shitty Luck. One guy just called it City Shit.

I wanted to include a chapter on food because I found that I had to learn very quickly the norms about lunch rituals in different countries (bringing your own lunch; buying a quick sandwich; eating at a restaurant; taking no break, a short break, a long break) and in different companies (eating together; eating solo; eating while working).

While offices can be mostly rather informal, the formality heightens when a client is around. At a more formal lunch, good table manners are noticed. I've been in some places where after a meal all diners discreetly use toothpicks right at the table. (You don't have to do that, but don't be grossed out if you're not used to it.)

So put your napkin on your lap, and let's dig in.

Eating with Others

Some etiquette consultants train people in companies to know how to distinguish a shrimp fork from a salad fork. In some cases (a formal dinner at a seafood restaurant, say) it actually may be important to know the distinction between those two pieces of cutlery, though I guarantee most diners really won't know or care which is which. But a problem could arise if you order a shrimp salad. Are you supposed to eat the shrimp with the shrimp fork and the salad with the salad fork? It would take a lot of dexterity to separate any green stuff that's clinging to the shrimp. What would happen if the shrimp fork actually touched a piece of watercress? Will people take out their phones and share your faux pas on Instagram? Will you be asked to leave the restaurant?

Calm down. The chef won't come out of the kitchen, see your grave error, and then suddenly don his coat, run through the dining room, and quit, all the while mumbling something nasty in French. At least I didn't see that happen when I used a steak knife one time to butter a roll.

In all likelihood, you'll have some food with people you work with. Sometimes it will even be free and provided for you, so just keep your mouth shut both when you're chewing and when you have dietary restrictions or food aversions. Push things you can't eat delicately to the other side of the plate. Note, though, that if you do have dietary restrictions of any kind, you should tell the person doing the ordering so the next time you won't be embarrassed walking around with just a plate of cucumber slices.

Dos and Don'ts

Surprisingly, young professionals ask me about what they should (and should not) do when they're eating with their bosses or colleagues. Even if eating together seems like something outside of the work you do, you likely spend enough time with coworkers that they've at least seen you take out your lunch. Much like everything else you do at work, the way you approach eating sends a message to people. From what you eat to how you eat it, someone will inevitably notice. (Ew, that guy just put ketchup on lo mein!) Here are some basic dos and don'ts. Consult an etiquette expert if you want more detail.

For example, a big do is to always show good manners, because there are manner nerds out there who might come from the same stock as the grammar nerds I mentioned in the grammar section. People may make judgments about you if you pick up individual linguine strands between your thumb and forefinger, slurp them down loudly, belch, and say, "Let's hear it for the champ!"

Even if you've brought food from home or a take-out place and are having an informal lunch with your team in a conference room, don't be a slob or champ. Good manners means:

- Sitting up straight
- Having a napkin on your lap
- Using utensils if appropriate
- Not speaking with your mouth full
- Not grabbing a handful of anything shared (e.g., chips, nuts, or fries) and licking your fingers before digging in for more

Also, a big don't is to not be a pig. Free food is a wonderful gift for everyone, so be thankful. If you're at a reception buffet, don't let everyone see your desperation and enthusiasm by following the waiter with the hors d'oeuvres tray and taking three sliders, overfilling your plate, going back for thirds, asking for a take-home container, or discreetly stuffing rolls in your pockets, whispering to yourself, "Great; that will take care of breakfast tomorrow and Wednesday."

Here are more dos and don'ts.

Do: At a work lunch in a restaurant with the team, boss, or client, prepare to engage in light banter about food, restaurants, interesting news items, and work-related topics.

Don't: Talk politics unless you work in politics or are absolutely confident that you won't offend anyone.

Do: Keep your mouth shut if coworkers spend part of the mealtime talking badly about someone.

Don't: Share pictures of any businesspeople you're dining with at a restaurant unless you get their permission. And certainly don't brag on social media about a famous person you dined with. Social media should mostly be about your private life. (See the next chapter.)

Do: Let the person who is doing an advance order for everyone know about any dietary restrictions so people don't have to go out of their way to cater to you at the venue.

Don't: Complain if you're served something that you're allowed to eat but don't particularly like; do your best to eat what's in front of you.

Do: Volunteer to help clean up if the lunch is informal and in your offices.

Don't: Ever order the most expensive item on the menu. The three-pound lobster sounds good, but a grilled cheese sandwich can also satisfy lunchtime belly cravings. Even if you're on an expense account, someone can still challenge your order of unlimited barbecued chicken wings.

Do: Be prepared to pay for lunch just in case your boss is a tightwad and expects you to pay for the three-pound lobster you ordered because you didn't read the previous don't.

Shouldn't Boss Pay for Lunch?

Dear Someone Else's Dad,

My boss just took me to the local deli for lunch. Nice time; very

continued

informal. The check came, he picked it up, looked at me, extended his hand, and said, "Eleven bucks." I gave him cash, he paid the bill, and we left. Shouldn't he have treated me? After all, it was only eleven bucks.

Thanks,

Down $11

Dear Down,

Unless he said, "Let me buy you lunch," he really wasn't obligated to pay for both of you. Even though I think it's a good practice for bosses to buy juniors lunch every once in a while, I can't expect others to think the same way. Just look at the experience as a not very expensive chance to have some private time with your boss. At least now you know what to expect when he invites you again.

Here's the bottom line about food: Enjoy the perks of any free meals but be grateful and polite. Also, don't always expect there to be a free lunch.

The Office Kitchen

Appreciate whatever perks are offered to you in your company kitchen. Some places only provide coffee, others add fruit, and others will have an entire array of cereals, snacks, beverages, candy, you name it. I've also seen places where the company provides some of those items but asks for a donation—maybe a dollar per item.

A big gripe in every office I've been in is what to do with personal food left in the refrigerator. Think about it: You brought your own food for lunch on Monday, but a client suddenly asked you to lunch. You're on the road Tuesday through Thursday, and by Friday evening, you forgot all about Monday's lunch decaying in the fridge. In the meantime, mold has started to grow on your strawberries, and no one wants to go near the strange glow coming from your plastic container. People wonder whose science experiment is inside the container. Finally, someone will put up some sort of an officious sign on the front of the fridge, saying, "All unclaimed food containers will be disposed of by tomorrow at 5 PM!" At that point, you remember that you're an offending party, or you just decide that the officious person will come with a hazmat suit and toss your lunch detritus into a nuclear waste disposal site. Here's what I recommend: don't be the jerk who leaves rotting food in the shared refrigerator.

Some offices have cleaning staff or designated employees that will collect stray dishes and put them in the dishwasher. (If that's the case, be sure to thank them regularly.) Other places are more similar to your home; if you leave a dirty dish in the sink, don't expect anyone else to clean it for you. Get to know best practices by asking administrative assistants, who often know the rules. Just because a coworker says, "You can leave that coffee cup in the sink; someone will take care of it," doesn't mean it's the proper thing to do. Putting your dirty stuff in the dishwasher doesn't take a lot of effort.

Messy Kitchen, Nasty People

Dear Someone Else's Dad,
How can we get people to clean up after themselves in the office kitchen?
Thanks,
I Hate Messy People

Dear Messy,
This is a common problem. 1) Don't send a passive-aggressive email ("Someone left a smelly spoon . . ."), send an angry email ("This is now the THIRD time I've . . ."), or be a martyr and clean things up

continued

for them and then expect their thanks. 2) Do put a sign over the sink reminding people that no dishes or glassware can ever be left in the sink because we don't have a cleaning person on staff, notify your manager or HR rep to deal with repeat offenders, and if repeat offenders are friends, remind them of the policy in person.

Eating in an Open Workspace

If you have your own office, feel free to stink it up with whatever food you most enjoy. You can even keep the doors and windows closed so the odors stay in there and permeate your furniture, clothes, and anything else that's lying around. And why not discard your used food containers and beverage cans and bottles right on an empty chair too? Someone will clean it up at some point. It may have worked great this way when you were in college, and you can do the same thing at work if you have your own office. It's a choice.

However, if you eat in any shared space (office kitchen, conference room, communal worktables), be smart about food odors, messes, and coworkers' food allergies. A person with a peanut allergy might go into a wheezing fit just because you spilled some peanut M&Ms on the floor. Another person might be repulsed by seeing a grease stain on an important paper. Others might gag at the smell of fish emanating from the microwave. Finally, some will be angered by discovering a large, empty pizza box sitting atop a small wastepaper basket while the big trash bin is just around the corner in the kitchen.

I'm not giving specific advice. You can probably figure out what to do based on my passive-aggressive mutterings. Just know where extra garbage bags and cleanser are kept.

New Associates, New Cuisines

Dear Someone Else's Dad,

I don't mean to sound intolerant, but we have a lot of new foreign employees who bring their lunches every day and heat them in the microwave. Honestly, the smell of fish or bizarre spices is something I haven't gotten used to, and the whole office kitchen and lunch area reeks. Can I ask people to be considerate of those of us who don't like that type of cooking?

Thanks,

Fed Up

Dear FU,

Nope. Part of working in a global workplace is getting used to and respecting others' habits, including what they eat. You have a choice: you can tolerate the smell of foods you don't know and at the same time get to know your new coworkers, or you can eat elsewhere and maybe alienate people from different cultures. You can, however, post a sign asking people to please spray down the inside of the microwave after using it, so one person's lunch flavors don't mix with flavors of the next person's lunch.

I am fascinated by different cultures, especially as they relate to food. I love going to São Paulo on business and having wonderful restaurant buffet lunches where everyone takes their time to enjoy each individual course. I love walking through underground passages in Tokyo where the restaurants display plastic versions of the lunches they are offering. I love getting a quick sandwich and crisps at Pret in London. I love going to Paris because, well, it's Paris.

In the US, there is no norm, but you'll learn how to adapt by seeing what other people do. So enjoy your food, and don't speak with your mouth full.

Nine

KEEPING YOUR DIGITAL AND PERSONAL LIFE PRIVATE

Even though you will work very closely with your colleagues and may eventually consider them close friends, I recommend that you think a bit about how much personal information you divulge about yourself early on. That's not to say you shouldn't feel free to tell people where you're from, where you went to school, what type of foods you like, etc. But until you feel comfortable sharing, hold off on talk about personal relationships, political or religious beliefs, and even the things you do for fun. Maybe you'll never feel comfortable sharing, which is OK too.

In one of her routines, comedian Amy Schumer says she took her mother to a soccer game so she could teach her about boundaries. I thought that was pretty funny, and I only wish that when I was younger, I had been a) more athletic, and b) wiser because I could have taught my mother that same lesson. Even if you have no trouble setting boundaries with your parents about what they know or don't know about your personal life, you should remember that very fuzzy and often invisible lines can exist between people's professional and personal lives.

You should be open with people about basic issues in your private life that may affect your time in the office—caring for an ill relative, picking up a child at daycare, dealing with a medical condition. Managers should know about these issues so that they won't be surprised if you have to run out in an emergency. But your job is to have managers remember that you do terrific work in spite of anything that gets in the way.

The following advice gives you some tips on keeping your online and real-life, or analog, personal information under control.

The Digital Side

I am not a stalker, but I have certainly googled people I've met in business to find out a bit about their backgrounds—mostly work history, interviews, articles, and so on. Without any additional effort, though, I've discovered where some live, what political campaigns they've contributed to, the clubs they're members of, messy divorces they've been involved with, etc. I've also come across pictures of them that I wish I'd never seen.

There's some stuff out there that you can't control, especially if you're a well-known figure in your field. But because social media has pervaded both our personal and professional lives, you have some choices about what information you want out there.

I'm not going to go into how to control your privacy settings on Twitter, Instagram, and Facebook—you can find out how to do that yourselves—but I highly recommend that you make your accounts as private as possible. Even seemingly innocuous pictures of you at a beach can give people instant impressions of the friends you hang out with, your favorite alcoholic beverage, your idea of casual attire, and your physical fitness level—all fodder for others' unfair value judgments and fair game for gossip.

Basic Guidelines

Facebook friends and Instagram contacts should be real friends and maybe family members. Ignore requests from people you work with, colleagues, and clients. I stupidly added and accepted friend requests from anyone I knew when I first joined Facebook. I eventually started "unfollowing" the businesspeople I had become "friends" with once I realized that I really didn't need to know all about their kids' baseball games, family reunions, and amazing cheesecake slices they had at the most beautiful resort in Bali.

Make sure you control who can tag you in photos and be smart about posting them to your news feed. You may not be able to control your friends' abilities to post a picture on their news feeds of you participating in a college beer-chugging contest, but you can keep it from showing up on yours.

Use LinkedIn as a way to connect with fellow businesspeople, and only post information that relates to work issues.

Open nonpersonal Twitter, Instagram, and Pinterest accounts for charities, e-commerce sites, brand building, etc. You can choose whether to invite business colleagues to view those posts if you think they will specifically interest them. I wouldn't ask work colleagues for money to support a cause unless you've spoken with them first. It can be embarrassing for everyone if you ask work friends for Kickstarter funding or charity donations. You don't want to feel obligated to give to others, and they should feel the same way about you.

New technologies, which pop up all the time, give more companies, advertisers, and even the public the chance to find out about your personal preferences. You have the right to privacy, and I recommend thinking clearly about any repercussions that could arise if even some of your information were out there. Choose wisely.

The Analog Side

Let's explore in-person connections through the following scenes.

Scene 1: Int. Office kitchen. Monday morning.

Terry: Do anything fun this weekend?

Riki: That's really none of your business.

Terry: OK, sorry I asked. I'll never ask you again about anything nonwork related. Goodbye and have a nice life.

Scene 2: Int. Office kitchen. Monday morning.

Terry: Do anything fun this weekend?

Jili: Oh. My. God. It was totally amazing. On Friday night
I went to this bar with some friends? And then this whole
gang of college friends of one of my friends got there, and
we all hit it off really well? So we literally stayed there till
about 2 AM doing shots; then we all Ubered to another
bar uptown, which we ended up closing. Then I did this
5K race and got like literally the worst oozing blister in the
world on my big toe.

*Scene continues even though Terry has quietly gone back
to work and has suddenly been replaced by Horiss, who
just walked in to grab a coffee but found himself trapped
between the refrigerator and Jili.*

Scene 3: Int. Office bull pen. Day.

An official-looking narrator walks in and speaks to no one in particular. People working in the office behind him wonder who he is, whom he's speaking to, and why a spotlight suddenly shines on him.

Narrator: Remember this: You don't have to be obnoxious and standoffish like Riki, who will forever remain an enigmatic coworker about whom people will likely murmur, "What a weirdo. I asked him if he wanted a glass of water, and he told me that was a personal question." And you don't have to be an oversharer like Jili, who turns a simple request like "Can you please hold the elevator door?" into an invitation to tell you about how she fantasizes that she could be stuck in an elevator one day with George Clooney.

Scene 4: Int. Office bull pen. Day.

Curtain lowers. We hear workers behind curtain saying things like, "When did we hire a narrator?" "Who's he talking to?"

There's nothing wrong with telling people about a restaurant you went to, a museum you visited, a concert you attended, a sporting event you participated in, even a religious service you went to. But be careful about the level of detail you provide. "I went to the amazing 17th-century Dutch painting exhibit" is innocuous. "I went to the amazing 17th-century Dutch painting exhibit where I had a huge fight with my father about how much money I make" is TMI.

Here are some topics you may want to avoid at work:

- Religion
- Politics

- Gossip about coworkers
- How much you paid for your vacation
- Your financial portfolio
- Conflicts with your spouse
- Your sex life
- The same topics above as they relate to others you work with

Here are people you should watch what you say with:

- Everyone

Look, I'm not suggesting you only talk about the weather or the food in the cafeteria with your colleagues, but I want to put up some warning flags about topics that may affect how people treat you. I hope that everyone has the opportunity to work in an environment where diversity of culture, experience, and thought are valued and shared. Just watch what you share.

Your Workspace

One last comment about keeping things private. You can tell a lot about people by what they choose to place around their offices or workspaces. Traditional old-fashioned partners' offices are adorned with pictures of their extremely happy and extraordinarily attractive families on ski trips, rafting adventures, beach holidays, animal-tossing events, etc. You may notice other things—a model of a prized sailboat, a collection of expensive guitars, maybe a framed, signed letter from a politician. I leave it to you to create your own stories about any of those traditional partner types.

You also might see admins' workstations with personal family photos, a tacked-up greeting card or two, and maybe a religious symbol of some sort. Again, I'm just giving you facts so you can make assumptions about different people. How much information about yourself do you want at your workstation? What does the screensaver on your laptop say about you? I don't want to suggest that you be an anonymous clone worker with no personality. But as you've seen in the examples above, people can write stories with just a few clues.

In the end, you'll get a sense of how open you'll want to be about your personal life with coworkers. Just be careful how far you want to go. There's nothing wrong with talking about your love of horror movies unless you start to share the thrill you get seeing dismembered bodies. (Though if that sounds like I'm talking about you, you probably shouldn't be working with others.)

Please, No More Sports Talk

Dear Someone Else's Dad,

I am the only woman on my team, and each day when all of us juniors are in our conference room before our morning meeting, the guys just talk about sports. I have nothing to add, so I just sit there. One of the more decent guys told me privately that he thinks I should engage in their banter so people can get to know me and diffuse the assumption that I'm a "shy, lonely girl." I don't have any pictures on my desk, and I haven't told people much about my personal life, which is far from what the others assume about me. How should I handle this?

Thanks,

I'm Not That Shy!

Dear INTS,

As a man, I apologize to you on behalf of all others of my gender who are totally insensitive. You don't have to divulge anything you don't want to, but here's a situation where you may not want to perpetuate rumors about you. During the sports-talk fest, you could say that you didn't see the big game, but you did see a great movie, or went to an interesting restaurant, and hope that the decent guy you mentioned will help engage everyone else in a chat about great films or food. Know also that you don't have to prove or say anything unless someone says something condescending to you.

A Word about Dating Coworkers

In the #MeToo era, people are wary of having work romances. Some young people I've spoken with said they would under no circumstances date anyone from work. Some firms have policies prohibiting dating between coworkers. I understand why people are nervous about potential repercussions, but keep in mind that not all work relationships end in a lawsuit. Face it: most of your waking hours are spent at your job, and you might meet someone there who interests you.

If you meet someone at the office and you feel there is some mutual connection, you can slowly get to know each other a bit more. You might start with small talk mixed with work talk in the kitchen. A bit more of a chat in the lobby, elevator, coffee bar. If you feel more comfortable, you can decide mutually to meet for a coffee or a drink after work.

Experts in harassment at work have noted that what appeared in the press was all about relationships and power. I would stay away from any relationships that played into power: a boss dating an associate, for example. Otherwise, here's my advice:

- Be smart about everything you do and whom you do things with.
- Decide whether you'll be able to manage keeping a relationship secret and still do superb work.
- Think about how your personal and work life will be if you break up.
- Figure out if competition at work can lead to friction in a relationship.

I know many longtime married couples who met at work many years ago. People who are passionate about the same kind of work automatically have something in common, so it's natural that two people would enjoy each other's company. A potential danger could be if a relationship is based only on a shared love of work. Spending some time together outside the office gives people the chance to see if there are other common pursuits and values. I'm all for trying things out as long as no one is in any way taking advantage of the other person.

Teammate's Personal Life

Dear Someone Else's Dad,

I think one of my teammates and one of our managers are in a relationship. I've seen them together outside the office, and I've noticed that they share subtle meaningful glances in meetings. I worry that my teammate is making a mistake and will likely get hurt. Should I say something?

Thanks,

Don't Want to Be Nosy

Dear Nosy,

You are sweet to be concerned, but I'd recommend staying uninvolved. If, however, you see that work is noticeably suffering or you notice some unfair favoritism going on, you should document what you see and approach HR.

Office Parties

Sometimes you do have to mix work with pleasure at various business cocktail parties, celebratory lunches and dinners, and occasionally parties at a colleague's home. Most companies expect you to attend and enjoy your-self, which you should try to do. Just know that as much as you want to be yourself at all these events, be on good behavior. Even at a party where you want to literally or figuratively let your hair down, someone can take an unflattering picture of you, post it wherever people like to post things, and *boom!* Your reputation can be sullied overnight.

I've gone to scores of holiday parties, managers' and coworkers' wed-dings, new baby events, cocktail parties at bosses' newly renovated apart-ments, company softball games, poker nights, karaoke events, and other parties where people participate in cringeworthy activities (think weird food-eating events, not anything illegal or compromising).

If you're not sure how to handle yourself or what to do or not do, here are some guidelines.

Do attend events you're invited to unless they conflict with major per-sonal events or encumbrances (weddings, religious reasons, family obliga-tions, illness). I know you always go to Zumba class on Saturday morning, but your boss's wedding or company's community service event wins out.

Do participate in whatever you feel comfortable doing. If the com-pany retreat is a skydiving party, you don't have to participate if you don't want to. Then again, don't be a total wet blanket or eye-rolling complainer who mutters loudly that every event is stupid. Even if you don't want to jump from a plane, you can find something on the ground to do—give out prizes, search for missing bodies—to show you're part of the team.

Don't drink too much. There's usually some sort of alcohol at work par-ties, but watch yourself. I went to a client's Christmas party, and a guy I had worked with—and actually really liked—saw me and suddenly went into a drunken tirade of foul language directed first at me and then at everyone around him. It wasn't pretty. I have no idea if anyone recorded his antics and posted them, but I do know that he no longer works at that company. Hey, there's nothing wrong with having some cocktails or beers, but if people see irresponsible drinking, they link your behavior to irresponsibility at your job.

Don't feel you have to bring a date. Companies make it pretty clear if spouses or plus-ones are invited, but don't be pressured to invite someone, especially someone you don't know very well. I was a plus-one many years ago to a woman I knew. (I'm sure she was desperate and everyone else she called said no, which is why she settled for me.) I had a completely miserable time because I didn't know anyone, no one cared that I was there, and my date went off to hang with her work friends and left me by the cheese dip and chips (there wasn't a big budget for food).

Some companies do no-spouse holiday parties, which can be good (your spouse doesn't have to wear a fake smile all evening, you don't have to worry about introducing him or her to everyone, you can talk office stuff to your coworkers without translating) or bad (you have to spend even more time with your coworkers or you might see some inappropriate behavior between colleagues).

Do be polite, charming, and appropriately chatty with your bosses and their significant others, but don't monopolize their time.

Do buy gifts to weddings or other celebrations, but don't spend a lot of money if it's your boss's event. You could give a donation to your boss's favorite charity or find an appropriate gift on an online registry. Do not give cash.

Don't underestimate how stressful social events can be for you or some of your coworkers. If you see colleagues standing alone, make an effort to say hello and engage in some chatter. You don't have to spend a long time with people; just know that some people suddenly feel they're back in high school and revert to shying away from the center of the action.

My final don't: don't feel you have to stay to the bitter end of an event to prove that you're a good team member. Showing up, smiling, and participating as much as you're comfortable with will do the trick.

Sweaty at Holiday Party

Dear Someone Else's Dad,
At our holiday party, I ended up putting on my boss's suit jacket

instead of mine (we're very close to the same size, and it was dark) before I went out on the dance floor. I danced so much and got so sweaty that I soaked completely through the jacket. When I reached in the pocket to take out my handkerchief, I found his wallet instead, so I realized my mistake, left his jacket on a chair, found my own, and left. Should I have told my boss what I did?
Thanks,
Unfortunate Sweatball

Dear Sweatball,

If I were your boss and retrieved my gross and soggy jacket, I definitely would have wondered what had happened. It would have been nice to at least receive an apology note and perhaps an offer to take the jacket to the dry cleaner. Since you didn't do that, I still think a spoken apology is in order. Your boss may not take cash from you for the dry cleaning, but it's still worth offering.

Ten

HAVE A NICE TRIP

I have enjoyed traveling the world for my job because I've gotten to learn about new cultures, meet interesting people, and if there's time, do some sightseeing. Nevertheless, it's still business travel, which is exhausting, stressful, and punishing. Traffic to airports can make a short trip unbearably long, flight delays and airport security lines are maddening, and some newfound food options can cause your belly to rebel. And believe me, getting sick when you're on the road, especially when you're in a foreign country, is no fun at all.

You also may have to travel with colleagues or clients, which can tax your small-talk skills, add to logistical nightmares of coordinating getting to the airport for flights home to different cities, and make you realize after eating every meal together that you don't like spending more time than you absolutely have to with certain people.

Before you order room service, raid your hotel minibar, and take lots of selfies of your exotic food and locales, read on for some advice from a longtime road warrior.

Know Your Company's Travel Policy Well

It can be exciting to go on your first business trip on behalf of your company, but you'll learn quickly that business travel can be very different from leisure travel. First, even if you're used to using your favorite apps to figure out where to go, where to stay, and how to get wherever you want to go, you may encounter some corporate restrictions.

Some companies have very strict policies about your time on the road, so get to know what is and what is not allowed. I once attended a conference at a large resort where most people were shuttled around in golf carts. I thought it would be easier to ride a bike between venues, so I rented one for $10, which was later denied reimbursement because the fine print in the travel policy said that bikes came under forbidden recreation fees.

Here are some things that companies may have policies on:

· How you book your travel. Many companies insist that you use the company's travel portal or agent, which takes advantage of negotiated hotel rates, rental cars, and some air tickets.

· Who can fly business class or higher and on which routes.

· How much the company will allow per diem, which spells out how much you will be allowed to spend on meals (watch out for room service charges!), tips, and ground transportation (some policies even break down costs for how much is allowed for each meal). Think twice before opening the minibar and nursing that cute little bottle of Scotch, munching that giant-sized Snickers bar, or exploring that discreet "love pack." Since all will be itemized on your bill, which you'll have to submit for reimbursement, you don't want your operations person to send you an email saying, "Hope you enjoyed your 'lovely' time, but we're not paying for it, lover boy."

· How your behavior on the road on behalf of the company may reflect on the company. Taking clients out to a respectable restaurant and even to a show or concert may be allowed, but inviting them to a hot tub party may show bad discretion on your part and reflect negatively on the company.

· How you treat service staff. No one is below you, anywhere. Treat people with respect.

Boss Is Rude to Uber Driver

Dear Someone Else's Dad,

I was once in an Uber on a business trip with my boss (who's pretty high profile and recognizable), and the driver made a wrong turn, delaying our trip by maybe a minute. My boss started to yell at him, called him an idiot, said he had no respect for his customers, and vowed to rate him one star on the app. I sat there silently and uncomfortably listening to his tirade, which I thought was completely overdone. I kept my mouth shut, but I wondered whether I should have said anything quietly to my boss, since the driver might have recognized him and could have posted something nasty about him on social media. (Luckily, I never found anything.) Did I do the right thing?
Thanks,
Very Uncomfortable

Dear VU,

Sorry you had to sit through your boss's unraveling. You did the right thing by keeping your mouth shut. As much as he was wrong to treat the driver so horribly, you can't change his behavior. If the driver had posted something on social media, your boss would have had to suffer the consequences of bad publicity. The one good outcome is that you recognized that anyone's reputation—high profile or not—can plummet with one stupid action. I hope for your company's sake that its reputation isn't sullied by being associated with your inconsiderate boss.

Know Basic Etiquette When You're in Another Country

In the US, most businesspeople address each other by their first names, which may seem a bit awkward and highly casual to those who are accustomed to working in a more formal environment like Japan, France, or Germany. I recommend checking with your peers to find out what level of formality or informality is expected with your superiors and clients.

Handshakes are a universal greeting, but beware of formalities and informalities in different parts of the world. In some European and Latin American countries, kissing on the cheek between men and women and between women and women is common in business settings. Still, I always recommend that you let the local women take the lead; don't assume that all businesspeople there are ready for a smooch. If a woman does come close to give a kiss, turn your head to make sure you don't get any lip-on-lip action. Think of an air kiss with a little cheek grazing.

In Europe, customs vary by country. You'd never be expected to kiss at all in a German or UK business meeting; handshakes are expected. In Spain and Portugal, you may find businesspeople greet or say goodbye with two cheek kisses—first the right cheek, then the left. In Italy, it is usually first the left cheek, then the right. The French might go in for three or four alternating pecks.

In Japan, the bow is the standard greeting, and in formal meetings, the deeper the bow, the deeper the sign of respect. Japanese businesspeople appreciate the bow as a greeting from Westerners, but some may combine it with a handshake. The Japanese also have a formal exchange-of-business-cards ritual (which differs greatly from the sometimes callow US version of tossing business cards across a conference table and hoping they land faceup); in Japan, you would hold the top corners of your card between your thumb and forefinger of both hands and present the card to the other person. You will receive a card in the same way, and then you are expected to read it and comment on it. "Chemical processing. That is an interesting business." Don't worry about not being able to read Japanese: their business cards are usually Japanese on one side and English on the other.

You won't always know what to do in every situation, particularly if you work with people from many different countries. But, as I mentioned, it's a good idea to observe your coworkers and follow the cues for what seems to be acceptable.

Pitches in Japan

Dear Someone Else's Dad,

I was recently on a business trip to Tokyo, where I was presenting the same business pitch I have done elsewhere around the world. In every other location I've visited, the audience asked a lot of questions, which allowed me to customize the pitch to the local crowd and allay any local concerns. In Tokyo no one asked me a single question, so I ended up talking more than I usually do, and as a result, I have no idea how effective my pitch was. I even wonder whether they understood me. Did I miss some cultural cues? Thanks,
Out of Place

Dear OOP,

I can't speak for every Japanese audience, but it is true that many Japanese prefer to listen carefully and remain silent—even not asking any questions—during presentations. (I wouldn't worry so much about their not understanding your English; they wouldn't have hosted you otherwise.) Yes, you could have asked someone beforehand about what to expect, but I wouldn't sweat over that at this point. Right now, I'd recommend emailing a very polite and formal thank-you note (using the formal Japanese honorific last name-sana), recapping your points, offering to answer any questions and clarify any points, and requesting a follow-up conversation to discuss next steps.

Socializing with the Boss, Coworkers, or Clients on a Trip (or Anywhere)

Just as you should be familiar with your company's travel policy, you should also know your company's code of ethics (assuming it has one), because it may dictate how people who have a corporate ID are supposed to behave when doing anything related to work. I also want to point out that these tips apply to any kind of socializing you might be doing after work or on weekends. If you're traveling with your managers, other team members, or a client, you may find yourself in one of these situations:

1. Boss/client doesn't socialize. Coworkers don't socialize.

2. Boss/client doesn't socialize. Coworkers socialize reasonably (drinks and dinner).

3. Boss/client doesn't socialize. Coworkers socialize too much—lots of drinking and potential improper behavior.

4. Boss/client socializes with coworkers reasonably (drinks and dinner).

5. Boss/client socializes with coworkers too much—lots of drinking and potential improper behavior plus expectation that everyone will join in with what the boss or client considers a good time (think dog racing, mud wrestling, hunting bunnies, etc.).

Clearly the warning scenarios are numbers 3 and 5. Let's go through those.

Number 3. Bottom line: Don't get totally wasted on a business trip, and don't let yourself become someone who's an enabler (or seen as an enabler) of someone who does get totally wasted. Simple point to remember: when you are outside your home office and being paid by your home office to travel, you represent your home office in everything you do publicly.

In addition, avoid bad behavior-by-association. A young worker once emailed me because she was berated by a manager who had seen a picture of the worker next to a drunken coworker on a trip, and then told the worker that she should have been more of a responsible party. While I feel that the worker who wrote to me may have done nothing wrong, I'd recommend staying away from others demonstrating poor judgment and staying away from social media at such times.

Number 5. People who find themselves in this situation typically ask whether they should go along with the boss's escapades because they want to be seen as team players even if they don't really want to play along or they have a big FOMO. Some managers jokingly say, "Hey, guys—Vegas rules here, OK?"[2]

You know what? Vegas rules don't exist according to any law. You shouldn't feel you have to participate in any activity or attend any event that makes you uncomfortable. Furthermore, even if someone has said, "Vegas rules! Whoo-hoo!" you should document any behaviors that you feel are inappropriate, potentially exclusionary, or harassing.

If your company doesn't have a travel policy, I recommend that you make a private one for yourself. Avoid situations that make you feel uncomfortable, and never assume that nobody will ever find out about stupid behavior. Your bosses, clients, and colleagues may be terrific business role models, but seeing how they act out of the office may make you

---

2   "Vegas rules" is a lame shortcut of the lame phrase "What happens in Vegas stays in Vegas," which is a handy phrase for people who believe that in Las Vegas general moral conduct and/or normal and sane behavior rules are off. In other words, the phrase reminds the participants in a tacit agreement that no one will say anything to anyone else if someone happens to catch you biting heads off live chickens, spitting them out, taking off your shoes, and yelling, "Braise my toes and call me Betsy!" (I have no idea what that sentence means either.)

rethink whether they are life role models. Most people will be great in both ways, but keep your eyes open.

Do I Have to Play Golf?

Dear Someone Else's Dad,
A colleague of mine recently told me that when she met a client on a business trip, the client immediately asked her whether she was a drinker. When she said she was, the client said, "OK, I'm doing business with you from now on!" My colleague said she matched the client drink for drink at a bar till 4 AM. She also said she didn't mind her hangover, since she knew that client was going to sign a contract with her. When I told her I couldn't do that, she said that in our business drinking, playing golf, hunting, fishing, and even camping were critically important activities in cultivating and maintaining client relationships. Do I have to do all of those things to succeed?
Thanks,
Sort of a Homebody

Dear Homebody,
I don't want to make any judgment about your colleague's decision or the decisions of anyone else who feels comfortable participating in those activities, as long as they are legal and not life-threatening. However, I highly recommend that you play these games on your own terms. For example, if you're not a drinker but don't want to call attention to your nondrinking behavior at a bar, order a club soda or diluted cranberry juice so people could think you're having a cocktail.

Social gatherings with clients should be fun. Find someone with a common interest and suggest an outing related to it: ball game, karaoke, cooking lesson, volunteer work, nature trail or hike. The activity doesn't have to involve winning. If the client insists on an activity that makes you uncomfortable, speak to your manager about why you're uncomfortable and suggest an alternative.

Road Warrior Tips

Like many other road warriors, I've learned how to make life a bit easier. Here's a list of recommendations and other things to consider if you're going to be doing a lot of traveling for work.

Airport lounge access	Don't expect your company to provide this perk or your boss to invite you as a guest. It's completely up to you if you want to invest in a credit card or other program that provides lounge access.
TSA PreCheck and equivalents	US residents should do whatever they can to avoid long airport security lines. Joining TSA PreCheck, Mobile Passport Global Access (which includes TSA PreCheck), or Clear can save you time going through security and coming back into the US.
Airline/hotel room upgrades	If you travel a lot and stay loyal to an airline or two, you may get upgrades (one extra bag free, priority boarding when you enter the gate on an actual red—or what once looked like red—carpet) based on your status. I recommend joining lots of airline frequent-flier and hotel brand points clubs and downloading their apps because they're all free, and you never know when you might get a little extra treatment with a dedicated member line, especially when your travel is delayed. Keep your personal information up-to-date in your airline apps, and make sure to enter your TSA PreCheck number where it says, "Known Traveler Number" so your boarding passes will automatically say, "TSA PreCheck."

Airline seat assignments	SeatGuru.com lets you plug in your flight and date and presents a map of your plane, letting you know the better, typical, and bad seats on that flight. Pick your seats accordingly on the airline's website or app.
Airline meals	Unless you're flying in business class or higher or are on a very long flight, pack something to eat so you can stay on a normal meal schedule.
In-flight Wi-Fi	Many airlines have in-flight Wi-Fi for purchase. You should show good faith to your company by being online, working, and available if you're on a day flight.
Checked bags	Do whatever you can to pack light and not check luggage, which can slow you and your team down if you're traveling together and can add an additional headache to your flight.
Difficult passengers/ hotel guests	Don't be one. Period. You're not more important than anyone else who is traveling and has to reach a destination for whatever reason.
No-foreign-fee credit card	If you can't charge everything on your corporate credit card when you're traveling internationally, I highly recommend getting a personal credit card that doesn't charge additional foreign-exchange fees. You'll be surprised how those fees on other cards can add up.
ATM card	Call the number on the back of your card to see which foreign bank ATMs will honor your ATM card without additional fees. Also notify that bank that you'll be traveling and using the card so your card doesn't get rejected or eaten by a local ATM.
Cash	Most places take credit cards, so you don't need to carry a lot of cash, but you should get some for non-ride app taxis and tips; in the US I leave $5 in my room each day for the housekeeping staff along with a "Have a nice day and thanks!" note. I leave an equivalent amount in other countries. When I check out of a hotel, I pay my bill with the remaining local currency I have left and then charge the balance to my credit card.
Tipping	Check travel websites to see what norms are in the country you'll be visiting. In the US we tend to tip more than people do in other places. In Japan tipping is considered extremely rude.

I'll update more on my website, and I welcome other suggestions.

Can My Partner Tag Along?

Dear Someone Else's Dad,

Can I bring my girlfriend on a business trip? The meeting is in a cool city, and the hotel is supposed to have a nice spa, so we thought we could stay on a few days after my business meeting is over.

Thanks,

Roadie

Dear Roadie,

I don't know what your company's policy is on bringing guests along on trips, but based on my experience, I'd say that bringing a companion is fine with two caveats:

1. Keep excellent accounting on what extras you charge to the room (spa services, premium movies, room service for two, minibar purchases), and make sure those fees are not passed on to your company for reimbursement.
2. You're at the meeting for work, so during meetings and meals, you must be fully present and willing to do what's expected of you. Make sure your girlfriend is aware that she may be spending a lot of time alone. Staying a few days more could be fine if the days are over a weekend or if you've planned them as vacation days. If you're planning on staying at the same hotel after your meetings are over, get two itemized folios when you check out—one for the workdays and one for the vacation days.

Eleven

MANAGING MANAGERS

Ideally, you'd like to have a good relationship with your higher-ups. You don't have to be BFFs with your manager—in fact, you shouldn't be—but you should strive for a relationship where your manager trusts that your interests are aligned. For example, you should try to anticipate what information your manager needs before meetings, or do deeper research on topics you know she is interested in.

Just as we analyzed audiences in previous chapters, learning about your manager's likes, dislikes, and goals is critical. Part of your manager's goals could come from mandates she has from her superiors. Getting to know the most senior executives' priorities is another topic you should master.

In this chapter, I'll cover how to manage relationships with managers' admins, how to prepare for a performance review, and how to ask for a raise.

Get to Know the Gatekeepers

One of the best ways to gather information on managers' likes and dislikes is through their administrative assistants, now mostly called admins.

Maintaining good relationships with admins is critical; they are typically very busy, so if you come off as demanding, they may not respond in what you consider a timely fashion.

Never be condescending ("You probably wouldn't understand this technical language") or overly solicitous ("My, that is a lovely sweater you have on; I'd love to get one just like that for myself/wife/mother/girlfriend/child so she'll look as beautiful as you"). If you ask for something, be sure you give the reason why and demonstrate how you can work together ("I'm hoping to get as much information from NAME OF IMPORTANT PERSON so that NAME OF ANOTHER IMPORTANT PERSON will be able to present it to NAME OF MAJOR CLIENT at the UPCOMING MAJOR EVENT THAT EVERYONE KNOWS ABOUT. Can you help me out or point me in the right direction?").

Admins typically keep their managers' schedules, and they can be very helpful in letting you know what is on their bosses' minds and how they like to receive information. Again, you don't have to be their best friend, but you can learn a lot by asking specific questions.

Complaining Admin

Dear Someone Else's Dad,

I have been trying to befriend a colleague's admin so she can help me coordinate an event where my colleague will be speaking. The admin has been mostly helpful, but now that we're "friendly," she feels free to complain to me about her boss and how she hates everything she has to do for him (just work stuff, nothing inappropriate). Plus, she uses the most foul language (not that I'm a prude or anything). How should I respond?

Thanks,

Bad "Friend"

Dear B "F",

Try not to pursue details about the bad stuff she's talking about, and certainly don't try to fix it. Just respond by acknowledging her feelings about being overworked ("Wow, it sounds like you feel really overwhelmed"). If she does ask for advice on how to deal with her manager, you can refer her to HR—it shouldn't be your job to solve any of her problems.

Your Performance Review

At some point, you're going to get a report card of some sort. Usually it's in the form of a sit-down meeting with your supervisor to go over how you've been doing. Some places ask employees to do a self-review, both qualitative and quantitative, so managers can comment on your self-perception versus their reality.

Reviews typically occur annually, though some companies conduct them semi-annually or even more frequently. In the most evolved companies—those that foster open communication throughout the organization—performance reviews occur spontaneously throughout the year.

I don't know anyone who doesn't get nervous before these meetings because we all fear knowing what others think of us. In addition, because performance reviews are often tied to raises, people focus on literally how much they are valued, which can involve an element of surprise. There is conventional and unconventional web advice on dealing with nervousness: deep breathing, meditation, crystals, juice cleanse, yoga, spin classes, forced smiling, forced crying, eating slower, talking slower, quiet room, primal scream, cucumber mask, or making animal noises (not a complete list).

I do recommend that you not pass on your anxiety to your parents, especially those of the helicopter variety. I'm always happy to hear when young people have swell relationships with their parents. Unfortunately, I also hear about parents who love their kids so much that they become invested in their adult children's careers—and by "become invested," I mean calling their bosses and showing up at their offices. This behavior is not healthy, is frowned upon by everyone at work, and makes you look immature. Whew, were those strong enough points to help you convince Mom to get out of the helicopter?

Preparing for Your Performance Review

Ideally, you shouldn't have any big surprises at your review. In any case, here's how to prepare:

1. Make a detailed list of all tasks you've completed successfully since your last review. It's an added bonus if you can quantify any revenue gains, expense reduction, or efficiency increases related to the work on this list.

2. Make another list of the skills you have been working on to enhance over the past year, including any skill level mastery. Then, plot out how you will continue enhancing skills next year. It's an added bonus if you include skills that your manager suggested you should improve.

3. Make a list of the projects you envision working on in the upcoming year that will raise your profile and that of your team. Another good idea is to identify people on your team you'd like to have exposure to.

During the Performance Review

Let's say your manager says, "Just one thing to work on this year: try to speak up more in meetings. But otherwise, you've demonstrated accomplishments in ten different areas! Everyone loves you! Never have we had such an amazing employee!" You'll leave the room despondent, thinking, "That jerk thinks I'm too quiet at meetings. I'm a total failure."

People tend to remember the first thing and the worst thing. In the case above, these items were the same. While the boss was hammering home what a great job you did in everything else, your mind was focusing on how people everywhere are talking about what a quiet mouse you are. Maybe they're laughing behind your back too. "There's the kid who doesn't say anything." "Oh, I've heard about you—you're the one who's so quiet; nice to meet you. Don't worry about saying anything back. Ha ha." In the meantime, you missed all the good stuff your boss said.

So, I offer you a few pieces of advice:

1. **Take notes.** Do it on real paper rather than on your computer so your boss can see what you're writing.

2. **Paraphrase.** To make sure your boss knows that you're comprehending everything, try to say, "OK, gotcha, you're saying that . . ." Paraphrasing is especially important when your boss talks about specific action items you're supposed to follow through on.

3. **Ask for items to work on.** Yes, I just said that in the previous bullet, but if your boss doesn't mention items to work on, make sure you leave the room with something tangible.

After the Review

Take a few minutes to absorb what you talked about. Don't call your mom. Once you process everything, look at your notes to make sure you've documented the important points. Don't call your mom. If you'd like, you can email your boss a summary of your review. Don't call your mom. Go home. Call your mom if you want, but remind her that she can't 1) call your boss, 2) email your boss, 3) text your boss, 4) visit your boss, or 5) threaten your boss.

The bottom line: Ask for feedback during the year so you can stay on track with what's expected of you. Listen carefully and paraphrase what you hear. And send your mom on a nice vacation where she can't receive calls or emails.

I Am Not Abrasive!!

Dear Someone Else's Dad,

I just received the results of a "360 review" in which a consultant asked everyone in our small company about my strengths and weaknesses. I was absolutely shocked to learn that no one here likes me very much. They think I'm "abrasive" and "way too intense," among other adjectives. I have done so much to help the company succeed, and now I feel like I've been kicked in the stomach. I took two personal days to absorb all of this. Should I just quit?

Thanks,

Stomach Plowed

Dear Stomach,

I'm so sorry that you feel hurt. I detest feedback that's full of adjectives, because they immediately put people on the defensive. Quitting may be rash. I would talk to the consultant and ask for very specific examples of how your behavior affected others. Listen carefully to understand why people felt the way that they did and ask for advice on techniques to help you handle situations like those differently. Perhaps you can talk to a manager about what you learned and how you will plan to change. Finally, if you have actually done good things for the company, I would hope that someone acknowledged them in the review. When you hear so many negatives, it's hard to focus on any good stuff.

Twelve

DIFFICULT PEOPLE SITUATIONS

Here's a question I receive a lot: "What do I do when my coworker/boss/ manager/admin doesn't stop/won't ever/is so/refuses to _____, which can be very distracting/obnoxious/rude/maddening?"

Conflicts are a fact of life at work, unless you work in a place where everyone's brains have been sucked out and exchanged for a chip that makes them productive, nice, happy, and humorless. Don't tell me you work there already.

I'll admit it: I am conflict-averse. And please don't argue with me, OK? My natural instinct is to defuse contentious situations with humor, which might make people chuckle for a bit but does nothing to resolve difficult issues. In business, though, addressing conflicts and finding ways to solve them are crucial; otherwise, negative feelings can fester, communication can fall apart, and efficiency and morale can falter. Leaders who would rather dig a hole in the sand and bury their heads to avoid conflict typically end up with a grumbly workforce and grains of sand in hard-to-clean orifices.

Before I give some advice on dealing with conflicts, please remember that conflicts involving harassment or harm of any kind should be reported to your superiors and to HR.

The types of conflicts I'll refer to are mostly ones involving competition, clashing egos, jealousy, and smelly foods left in the refrigerator. And the way to deal with most of them is to communicate quickly and concisely and focus on facts, consequences, and solutions that benefit all stakeholders. The way *not* to deal with conflicts is to let emotions take a back seat to savvy business decisions.

The High Road

No one has to live in a totalitarian regime, but having rules makes a difference. Children are taught and appreciate basic rules: "Use your words." "Hair pulling isn't allowed." "You can't say, 'You can't play.'" "Don't lend money to support your father's gambling habit." "Keep political arguments with your grandmother to a minimum, and don't hit her." These are standard.

Codes of conduct should be present in all workplaces, but surprisingly, I've worked with companies where rules aren't posted, and as a result, free-for-all behaviors are accepted (yelling all the time, withholding important information as retaliation, etc.). I hope your company's roles and rules are defined. If they're not, stick with the rules of basic human kindness, where taking the high road is at the top of the list.

Here's an example at a company with no code of conduct:

> Jer: Hey, do you know what happened to last month's audited numbers for the Chizwizz account? I can't find the file on the shared drive.

> Kyl: I was wondering when you would notice. I took it off the drive because you didn't tell me about the new compliance guidelines yesterday, so it's your turn to fly blind.

Jer: Don't blame me if you didn't read the email, you worthless, petty slop of thawing seepage.

Kyl: I'm afraid those are very inappropriate words to use in the workplace, you repulsive scum.

You can see where this is heading, and it's not pretty. A better response to the seepage person would be to focus on facts, take the high road, not go down to the base level, and kill them with kindness. Also, do not apologize for something you didn't do.

Here is a "high road" approach:

Jer: Hey, do you know what happened to last month's audited numbers for the Chizwizz account? I can't find the file on the shared drive.

Kyl: I was wondering when you would notice. I took it off the drive because you didn't tell me about the new compliance guidelines yesterday, so it's your turn to fly blind.

Jer: Oh my, I thought you received the email about the compliance guidelines too. I hope you didn't have to do double work; that must have been tough. Next time, please ask me if you feel you're missing something; I'll be happy to give any information I have. Really sorry.

Kyl: OK.

Jer: Anyway, can you please reshare the Chizwizz file? I was asked to put together a report by noon, and I'd hate to not meet the deadline, since I want our entire team to look good.

Notice how the focus stayed on the facts rather than emotion, provided a solution for potential future conflicts, and showed willingness to benefit the whole team. Here's another example with an accuser type:

> Dil: Hey, Nor, how was your weekend?

> Nor: Were you looking at things on my desk when I wasn't here?

> Dil: No, I don't think so.

> Nor: So you mean you may have, and you don't remember? Or you didn't look?

> Dil: Honestly, I don't remember needing to look at something on your desk, but that's not to say I didn't inadvertently glance at it when I was walking by.

> Nor: Well, let's just assume you did. Did you see my color-coded stack of Moleskine notebooks that I spent an entire week organizing? The red one is out of place! You can't trust anyone around here to leave your stuff alone! And if you even "glanced," you must have noticed!

Yes, people like that exist. The person is putting you on the defensive, so the more Dil engages with Nor, the worse it can get.

> Dil: I'm sorry, but I didn't notice, and please don't accuse me of messing with your stuff.

> Nor: Well, you're the obvious person who would have done something, since you sit right there.

Dil: (Sobbing) I swear I didn't! Maybe you just misplaced the red one.

Nor: You're saying it's my fault?

Dil: Why do you have to be so mean to me?

Nor: Me? Mean to you? Do you know how much I put up with?

I know you'd like to know what happened next, but that will be in the forthcoming volume, tentatively entitled *Battle of the Nobodies*.

Here's a better way of handling the situation, again just by sticking to facts and acknowledging Nor's feelings:

Dil: Wow, sounds like you're upset. I know how much time you put into organizing those notebooks.

Nor: You bet I did! Do you have any idea what could have happened?

Dil: I wish I did. What a bummer.

Again, see the sequel to find out what happened.

My Shoes, Your Shoes, and Compromising

When you're in a conflict, try to put yourself in the other person's proverbial shoes. What is the person's motivation? Why does that person care? How much do you care? Can you imagine a compromise where both of you are happy?

Spend some time plotting out what truly matters and figure out how much you will be willing to budge before you confront someone where a compromised solution would make sense. You don't want to be known as a person who always has to get your way. It's not an attractive quality, and you'll never be able to negotiate.

Here's a simple workplace example:

> Mol: You talk so loud on the phone all the time that I can never concentrate on my work.

> Ven: You could just buy some noise-canceling head-phones and put them on when I'm on the phone.

> Mol: Or *you* could find another quiet office when you have to make a call and go there.

> Ven: Or *you* could go to that quiet office because I need to have my terminal in front of me when I do some of my calls.

> Mol: Fine! *I'll* buy expensive headphones, and *I'll* leave our office so *you* can have it *your* way!

Mol should have thought of a negotiating plan before confronting Ven.

> Mol: Ven, since we're sharing the office, I wanted to talk about how we can both be more productive. One issue is that you speak very loudly on calls, which affects my productivity. I came up with some solutions that might work for both of us.

> Ven: Like what? I don't think I can be softer; I've got a lot of people on my calls and people often have lousy connections.

Mol: If we share each other's calendars, we can see when your calls are scheduled, and we can decide in advance whether one of us can step out to another room.

Ven: I need to have my terminal in front of me when I do some of my calls.

Mol: Right, so with those calls I can find another place to work, but with other calls you can call from another office. Just trying to be fair.

I am definitely turning these two characters into costars of a sitcom. I know a lot of people who may be perfect fits for the roles.

Parenting Rules Work Well

Conflicts are a good thing because they force you to resolve issues and help you understand others. But don't try to take every conflict and turn it into a lesson on how we all should play well together in the sandbox. ("OK, everyone, what's our valuable lesson for today? Dave?") While some conflicts can seriously impede the progress and effectiveness of your team and should be addressed, others are merely the equivalent of having your little brother repeatedly poke your shoulder—it's annoying, but you can beat the crap out of him to make him—er, I mean it's annoying, but the behavior will eventually go away if you ignore it.

Pick your battles: address truly major issues and look for ways to resolve them and learn to live with minor grievances.

I Want the Best Chair!

Dear Someone Else's Dad,

We used to have offices with nice views, but now we share long tables. My colleague was assigned the seat next to the window, which I thought was unfair, so we agreed to take turns at the window seat: Monday and Wednesday for me, Tuesday and Thursday for her, and on Fridays, whoever gets in earliest gets the seat. On Fridays, the two of us have a race to get there first, and it's getting a bit silly. Do you think this was the best way to resolve the seat issue?
Thanks,
Fair and Square

Dear Fair,

Honestly, the whole thing seems a little silly. The two of you have already gotten into a power play about a stupid seat. Is that the most important thing to be concerned about? Sure, the seat by the window has a nice view and affords a little more privacy, but is the non-window seat so bad that it's like you're sitting in an old bus station? One of you has to be the grown-up. Maybe you could have the window on alternate Fridays. Get to work.

Different People/Different Thinking

It's critical to develop techniques on how to deal with people different from you and disagreements that can impede the success of your team. Before we examine specific situations on how to deal with challenging people, let's examine people's differences.

Social Style Differences

Several social style tools (MBTI, HBDI, DISC, StrengthsFinder) assess people's preferences on how they react to different situations, including approaching tasks, dealing with other people, listening and responding, researching information, evaluating alternatives, and so on. The results—it could be an acronym, a color, or a descriptor, depending on the test—help you understand how to adapt your style when working with someone who is different from you.

The first advantage of these types of assessments is that they allow you to recognize that people with different strengths, styles, and ways of thinking can add a lot of value to a team. A second advantage is that when you become aware that people you deal with or need to persuade have different social styles from yours, you may begin to approach them in ways that match their ways of thinking.

For example, let's say your firm uses the Sea Creature Assessment Test (or SCAT) to determine social styles. After you fill out a long questionnaire, your profile is determined to be a crab—meaning you grasp things quickly and are able to move around to complete many tasks in a short period of time. Your colleague, Li, however, is a flounder, seeing things only from one side of her head and not open to new ideas. In order to persuade Li to change from keeping all client notes on separate local files to using a new shared platform that allows the team to collaborate, you would have to spend extra time with Li acknowledging the advantage of the old system and how it worked well in the past before you can broach the topic of the benefits of a new system.

Similarly, if you have to persuade Hali, another colleague, who is labeled a shark, or one who keeps moving without stopping until she smells trouble, you may have to get to the point quickly and make a pitch as you chase her around.

. . . .

Other SCAT Characters

Carp: bottom feeder, steals others' ideas
Whale: bloated worker who has been at the company too long
Minnow: follows whatever anyone else is doing
Salmon: enjoys dealing with obstacles, likes change
Anchovy: oily, unpleasant
Tuna: high self-worth, embellishes with cosmetics to make himself look better

. . . .

A drawback of social styles assessments is that the labeling can be a bit too rigid and may empower people to give excuses about why they aren't able to do something. ("Sorry, I don't provide new ideas. Remember, I'm a minnow.") Being labeled a minnow should make you realize that there's an opportunity for you to move beyond your comfort zone of being a follower. Also, a label may apply to you in only one area of your life; you may be a minnow when working on a neuroscience project but more of a tuna when you're doing a social media campaign for some way-cool shoes.

Finally, your style may change over time, though morphing into a bloated whale is not my idea of a life goal. Age, new situations, and experience may change your outlook on how you deal with issues. That anchovy may be able to turn into a salmon after all. I leave you with that slimy visual.

Cultural Differences

Why do I sometimes prefer to say what's on my mind without thinking first? Why do you mostly nod your head and smile instead of letting me know what you're really thinking? Why does that person over there enjoy engaging in banter about a wonderful meal he had and then ask you about your favorite food before talking about ideas? Why does that person like to ask rapid-fire questions? Welcome to Earth.

Our personal communication styles have been nurtured by our surroundings and by people who have influenced us. Consequently, people from different cultures approach social and business situations in different ways.

In the US, cultural norms may dictate how people work together. As I've noted before, I'm from New York City, where a "typical" native might be characterized as fast-paced, brash, and impatient. And just shut up if you don't agree with me. In the Midwest, the typical person is thought to be friendly, helpful, and patient. West Coast natives are supposed to be laid-back and carefree. These are huge generalizations indeed, but I want to emphasize that people who grew up in different surroundings bring a part of their native cultures to work each day.

Since events shape our personalities and cause us to respond to different stimuli in unique ways, those unique ways of responding can be irritating to people who approach the same stimuli differently. And as much as you'd like to shake someone and say, "What's the matter with you? Don't be that way!" remember that you really can't change other people, but you can change the way you respond. Let's call it the My Challenge Guideline (MCG).

Imagine being locked in a cage for ten hours every day with people of different social styles and cultural backgrounds and being told to be productive and happy. Following the MCG may not make things close to perfect, but you may have better insights on how to deal with conflicts that will inevitably arise.

Not Your "Typical" Foreigner

Dear Someone Else's Dad,

I'm an expat working in Silicon Valley for a big tech firm. My boss has a fancy sailboat that he loves to race. He often recruits some of us young guys to be on his crew during weekend regattas. When I asked him why he's never asked me to be a crew member, he said,

continued

"Oh, come on. You're not exactly the type who'd yell, 'Get out the #*$@-ing way, you ^#@*#-ing @*&^%#!'" I may be the quiet type in the office, but that doesn't mean I'm a typical passive foreigner. Should I ask my boss to include me next time?
Thanks,
Excluded Foreign Guy

Dear EFG,

It all depends on whether you really want to be a part of a crowd that yells, "Get out the #*$@-ing way, you ^#@*#-ing @*&^%#!" all afternoon. If you do want to be a part of the crowd because you honestly think it would be fun and you feel you can easily recite those words in a boisterous voice, you should make a case to your boss. I'm not recommending you prove it by yelling those words in his office or in an open bull pen (think of the weird looks you'd get), but you could say, "I'm up for the challenge. Just because you see me as a quiet type at work doesn't mean that when I'm out of my work clothes I'm not a big, bellowing competitor! Whoo-hoo!"

I'd recommend not bringing up the term "typical foreigner" unless you're comfortable saying it. You may want to write something to your manager and copy HR if you feel like the main reason you haven't been invited to be on the crew is because you are being discriminated against for being from another culture.

Types of Difficult Coworkers

From time to time, we all have to deal with annoying or disruptive people. For your sake, I hope you aren't surrounded by toxic coworkers. But when you meet one, you might as well know how to recognize the type and minimize conflict.

Know-It-Alls

The know-it-all (KIA) can be irksome on many levels. No matter what your background or expertise, rest assured that KIAs claim they know more about it than you do and can solve everything related to it. Here are snippets of conversations with different types of KIAs:

Type 1

Jim: I've been working on this project; I'd love for you to take a quick look when you get a chance to see if you have any comments.

KIA: Hmm. There are *so* many issues. You know, let me just start over and do the whole thing myself.

Type 2

Lil: I'm putting together a piece for our clients on the long-term effects of consuming more than three ounces of caramel brûlée latte topping per day.

KIA: Good idea, and you're actually very lucky because you just happen to be talking to the right person! I wrote a series of papers—for which I got funding from a very prestigious foundation that only gives out a handful of grants—all about how children's teeth can be destroyed by poorly made muffins. It was a game-changing study—quoted everywhere—and really affected the muffin industry. You'll be dealing with the absolute expert here if you need help. Happy to share my wisdom.

Type 3

Bette: I just met our new client, Dan Fann, who said—

KIA: Dan Fann! *Everyone* knows all about him. Very smart. Very well known.

Bette: Yes, and he said he can help us with our Asia strategy—

KIA: Of course, Asia is his specialty! He's the expert! I've talked about Asia with him many times!

Bette: Right, so he was saying that we should talk to his colleague Ron Konn about—

KIA: Ron Konn is the best. Great idea. Ron was a great hire for Dan. Excellent person.

Bette: Actually, I just made up the name Ron Konn. He doesn't exist.

[OK, I made that last line up. But I so wish it were true.]

Unfortunately, dealing with know-it-alls is tough because they are always going to self-promote, and there's no real benefit in calling them out. And as much as I'd like to say, "Ha ha, liar, there's no such person as Ron Konn," the KIA's comeback might be, "I knew that sounded wrong. There's another person on his team I'm thinking about, also named Ron, I believe, who's very good." You'd be stuck trying to figure out your comeback.

Remember, since you can't change the KIA's annoying personality, you just have to accept that you'll always get a KIA-type comment and not let it affect you that much. Take a deep breath, say, "OK," and move on.

Credit Hogs

People who take credit for your work are bad news. In addition to being self-promoting, they are insecure and insensitive. When coworkers or managers either deliberately or not so deliberately take full credit for a project you spearheaded or worked on, your reaction is likely to be somewhere between "Golly, I thought my name was supposed to be mentioned. Oh well, no big deal. It doesn't bother me, for after all, I don't deserve praise" to "Excuse me? What the *%$& just happened?"

The latter emotion is more common. And why not? We all want to receive appropriate credit for work we've done and feel upset when we don't get it. It's perfectly natural to feel angry, betrayed, and belittled. Still, you should approach the person who upset you to clear the air while the specific circumstances and emotions are fresh. But stick to the facts as much as possible, because accusing someone will only lead to denial from the accused and more stress for you.

Here's an example: Bo proudly mentions in a management meeting how he (without mentioning you) completed your study demonstrating that people who save their handmade aluminum foil balls are more likely to eat processed snacks packaged in aluminum foil. If you're thinking quickly, you could find a time to say in the meeting, "Bo is talking about the study I initiated back in April when I noticed that many hoarders of handmade aluminum foil balls also had an unusual excess supply of exact change, which I surmised could be used in candy machines. I knew it would be a great achievement to get to the bottom of this."

Instead, if you feel too wounded to say anything in the meeting, you should find a moment to talk to Bo in person and tell him what you heard and why it upset you. Remember, stick to the facts and how you felt. "Bo, I noticed that you said you completed the study on hoarders of handmade aluminum foil balls without mentioning me. I have to admit I was surprised and a bit hurt. Is there a reason why you didn't bring my name up?"

You can also set an example in other conversations by mentioning the contributions made by others to tasks you've worked on. ("Thanks to Rudda and Dudda for doing all the interviews.") Just try to keep some of the goodwill for yourself; you don't have to brag about what you've done ("Yes, I was the one who really saved the day!"), but you can say how proud you are of an outcome, especially if there is a tangible, quantifiable result.

In sum, if you have felt that your contributions have been minimized by others, make sure you find ways to receive the appropriate credit for your work.

Blamers

Another type of annoying person always looks for a specific reason for why something unexpectedly turned sour. In the blamer's eyes the reason always involves a person. The door mechanism didn't work this morning. Whose fault was that? Our sales numbers were down this month. Whose fault was that? It started to rain. Whose fault was that?

Obviously, many events are beyond anyone's control. But starting an argument with someone who fights against the world is fruitless. Some blamers also chronically make negative comments about people they think are perpetually at fault. My advice: Don't play along and argue unless you have facts to disprove their assumptions. Document what you hear, and then let HR deal with the blamers' insecurities.

In instances where another person indeed might have been at fault for causing a setback of some type, listen carefully to the blamer so you can separate facts from emotion. If you caused the problem, own up to it in person—not in an email, if possible—and again, focus on why it happened and apologize for any misdeed. Once any damage is done, though, all energy should be on how to move forward and how to learn from mistakes.

Here's an example of a blamer in a meeting:

> Flip: Before we proceed with our agenda topics this week, I want to point out a very grave problem. Correct me if I'm wrong, but I distinctly remember that we agreed we wouldn't discuss our Pribble negotiations with anyone

outside this room. I have learned that one of us has leaked critical information to a board member, which could possibly have deleterious effects and destroy our reputation completely. I don't want to say the name of the offending party, but I think we should hold a trial to get to the bottom of the leak and take punitive action.

Chip: The person you're referring to is me, but there was no leak. The board member asked me in the elevator how the negotiations were going, and I said they were moving along. That is all I said. I gave no details.

Flip: I consider that a breach, and we should do a full investigation into the event.

Chip: I just told you the extent of what happened. I'm sorry that you felt that it went against our agreement, but there was no harm done.

Flip: I move to ban this member from all future conversations; he clearly cannot be trusted. I feel a personal betrayal because of his sloppiness. Anything we decide together will be completely beyond his control. Anyone second this motion?

Silence.

Kip: OK, let's just make sure we respect the confidentiality of our conversations here. Let's get to our agenda.

Flip, the blamer, became caustic and a bit holier-than-thou. Fortunately, no one went along with his proposal, and people just moved forward because they stayed with the facts and didn't get swayed by Flip's emotions.

People with Bad Hygiene

Here's an issue that doesn't relate to personality. In fact, the person can be the nicest, most generous person in the world. But when other people notice a funky odor whenever the person comes near, the other people generally don't want to discuss the issue because it's awkward, personal, and embarrassing.

Still, I get this question a lot: How do I deal with a stinky coworker? No one wants to confront someone with bad hygiene, because no one wants to offend the person. But it's critical that someone tell the offending party about noticeable odors, because it makes others uncomfortable. Without getting into details, some people have no idea that they have body odors or that their clothes appear unwashed. My advice always is to make sure a manager is aware of the issue and agrees to say something to the person.

The message can be simple, but it should be face-to-face and behind closed doors. I recommend saying, "This is a difficult topic, but people have been noticing that you have some personal hygiene issues. I don't want to go into details, but I'm asking you to please take care of it. Got it? Thanks a lot."

Honestly, I don't want to get into more details because I'd rather not discuss reasons for bad odors. But odors also can come from excessive use of strong perfumes or colognes. I recommend handling this situation in the same way: bring it to a manager's attention.

Hoverers

Another difficult conversation to have is the one with coworkers or managers who linger around your desk and don't take a hint that you want them to scram. If a situation veers toward harassment, immediately talk to someone in HR. However, if the person likes to hang around to gossip or engage in innocuous, friendly banter, which can impede your effectiveness, here are three strategies.

· **Keep noise-canceling headphones on at all times.** Pros: no one will bother you since you're showing you're closed for business. Cons: people may perceive you as antisocial or anti-team, which may not be good for group morale.

· **Tell the person it's not a good time.** "Hey, this isn't really a good time for me to chat because I have to get this [name of extremely important project] for [name of very extremely important person] finished by [extremely impossible to achieve deadline]." Pros: the person will get the message that it's not playtime. Cons: the person might say, "That's OK, I'll just hang here till you're done!"

· **Show that you're glad the person is there.** Say you "need help with [most impossible project beyond the scope of this person's intelligence]." Pros: Best way to get rid of the person because you know he can offer no help at all and therefore will likely scurry along. Cons: The person offers ridiculous "help," which can allow you to say, "No, I guess you're not the best person to help on this." Then go back to your screen and watch the reflection of the person leave, dejectedly.

Those are good ways to get the annoying hoverer to find another place to annoyingly hover. Here's one more technique: when you see the hoverer come near, immediately pick up your phone and either have a pretend fight or feign absolute shock at what you're hearing. When the hoverer approaches, use a "shoo/go-away-right-now" gesture with your hand to protect your privacy. Disadvantage of this technique: the hoverer may stop by later to find out what happened.

Also, the modern open office can become very conducive to 24/7 play-time. Noise-canceling headphones, deathly glares communicating "buzz off," "Quiet Zone" signs, shoo-away hand gestures, and even whispering, "Hey, guys, I gotta get something done here; could you keep it down a bit?" may not stop the game of hacky sack going on behind you.

Finding a quiet space in the office could elicit a "What's the matter? Don't want to hang out?" message from even the most dedicated workers who feel that you should be able to work and play at the same time. Please don't be swayed by peer pressure. Find time to hang out when you can, but also find a way not to get into the hacky sack game.

- Work from home sometimes if you can. If being in the office is important, get work done quietly at home, then head into the office late in the day for face time.
- Work with your team to find a dedicated do-not-disturb zone.
- Organize a hacky sack tournament that meets at 3 PM in the parking lot.

It's a wonderful thing to have a team that likes to hang out together, but someone has to set the limits on playtime, work time, quiet time, and nap time. Good night.

We can all appreciate our diversity of backgrounds, cultures, ways of thinking, genders, and generations, but differences in personality types span all of these diversity levels. The best way to deal with people on the "difficult" part of the spectrum is not to get sucked into their manipulations. Stick to facts, be graceful, and learn how to adapt your messages to them based on how they process information.

Weirdo Manager

Dear Someone Else's Dad,

One of my managers is one of the weirdest guys I've ever met. He doesn't seem to do anything, never engages with the juniors, and when he does, he stares at us with a blank stare and goofy smile like he's totally stoned. The other day I asked him if he'd like me to include him on an email to a client, and he literally said, "Oh, what? Right. Yeah, sure." Should I report his behavior to someone? Also, what should I do if he asks me to be on a project with him? Thanks,

The Sane One

Dear Sane,

You seem to have great observational skills, and I encourage you to document anything you see the guy doing that is illegal or disruptive. But at this point you don't have anything concrete to complain about, and your conclusions are really all conjecture. Now, if you're asked to work with him, I would make sure you take copious notes on all details on any project, create a very detailed project plan, and make sure he clarifies all details. Be as professional as possible. This is all conjecture on my part, based on your assumptions that he'll be difficult to work with, but, hey, he might surprise you.

When to Approach HR

I've given you a lot of techniques on how to deal with difficult situations on your own. I've also mentioned some specific situations where you should get your manager or human resources representatives involved. Here are five areas where you might not want to talk to your manager but also shouldn't try to handle things by yourself.

When health issues affect your work. No one should ever pretend to be superhuman and work through any physical or mental illness. If your body is letting you down, make an appointment with the appropriate practitioner and decide together what course of action will move you in the right direction. Don't think it will be a sign of weakness to discuss serious matters with HR, especially if they relate to sick days or a reduced workload.

If you are harassed in any way. If someone touches, threatens, or harasses you because of gender, race, religion, ethnicity, sexual orientation, disability, age, or any other protected class, make a formal complaint to HR immediately. By law HR has to investigate these types of issues.

If you are discriminated against in any way. The same legal rules apply to the same classes noted previously. Make a formal complaint, which HR legally must investigate.

If you are uncertain about health benefits, insurance, vacation time, ADA compliance, or medical leave. Keep the word *resources* in mind. HR is a repository for all information related to your benefits and rights.

If the guidelines and suggestions I gave you don't work out. Hey, you gave them a try, right?

Dealing with Panic Attacks

Dear Someone Else's Dad,

I have a history of panic attacks that have prevented me from going to work at times. I have called in sick on those days, but I haven't explained to anyone what the sickness is, because I worry that people will think it's all in my head rather than the debilitating illness it truly is. I see a therapist about my issues, and I am working on techniques to deal with the attacks. How open should I be with people at work? I really don't want people to judge me as a crazy person.

Thanks,

Feeling Judged

Dear FJ,

I'm so sorry you're struggling. First, please know that it's against the law for companies to discriminate against any employee because of a mental illness, including panic attacks. Second, I think it's a good idea to be open with your managers and HR about your condition because they'll learn that the condition is real, and perhaps will understand better about anxiety and its manifestations. I'm not a therapist, so I can't give professional advice about your situation, but I am sure you're working with your practitioner on what likely triggers your panic attacks. You may want to explain to some people you work with what you may need to do (e.g., go to a private room) to calm yourself down. Lastly, please don't feel you're weak, blame yourself, or feel that you suffer alone. I've found that when I discuss mental illness in confidence with colleagues, they will often share the struggles they or their family members have had.

Thirteen

DIFFICULT CONVERSATIONS

My goal as an advice-giver is to provide people with techniques to manage their lives at work and help them achieve whatever goals they need to achieve. This often leads to conversations about people's professional aspirations and life goals. Many times, a certain job can fit perfectly on the path to someone's dream career. But I'm finding more and more that young people don't want just a job; they want experiences—working in remote locations, learning new languages and cultures, and sometimes just living life in nontraditional ways.

I'm all for that. Life is long, and I believe you can do what you want as long as you can cover your expenses, have a plan to deal with unforeseen medical costs, and can explain to your parents why you're doing what you're doing without having an argument.

Maybe the job you have isn't right for you, or maybe it's not right for right now. But letting your company know how you feel can be tough. I've put together two sections with advice on how to ask for time off and how to leave gracefully.

Asking for Time Off

Many companies have policies giving employees a chance to take unpaid leave for health reasons or skills enhancement, such as pursuing an advanced degree. Some companies allow people who have worked for a certain number of years an opportunity to take a limited-time sabbatical just to recharge. Smaller companies may deal with these issues on a case-by-case basis.

If you feel that you need a break, I would make a list of pluses and minuses about why you need to leave and the manifestations of each reason. Here's a table that may help you.

Reason for Time Off	Manifestation	How to Handle
Stress	Inability to work effectively; panic attacks; depression.	• See a therapist for a professional diagnosis. •Talk to your HR rep about medical leave. • Be open about what you and your therapist think is the best course of action in the short and long term.
Education	Professional skills need heightening to be more effective and competitive.	• Check company policy about education reimbursement. • Decide if part-time study can work for you. • Check for advancement opportunities following new degree.
Need to recharge	Overworked; not getting enough sleep; need to take care of yourself.	• See if you can take a few unpaid vacation or personal days. • Show commitment to your job and company. • Don't make this a habit.
Want to explore for a bit, but want to come back to your same job	Other friends quit their jobs to explore, but I want to know if I can come back. Plus my parents said they'd disown me if I didn't have a plan for later.	• Be honest about your plans. • Demonstrate the value you provide to the company (be specific) and your commitment to staying at the firm for a long time (and you should be honest about that too). •Weigh the option of being disowned by your parents (it could be a scare tactic).

I hope my advice for the last two cases doesn't cause a flood of people rushing to their managers' doors saying, "Please let me out of here so I can have fun, fun, fun for as long as I want, and I really, really promise to come back and work hard, hard, hard!" (That wasn't exactly my advice.) But you can ask yourself, "What's the worst that can happen if I ask?" The worst would be an answer like, "No, we can't allow that. And by the way, you're fired." Just decide whether you want to take that risk.

Use the table above as a way to think about approaching your company. Before you approach your supervisor and HR, check whether your company has any policies on sabbaticals or unpaid leave. There may be a formalized process that can help you determine the best plan of action.

If there isn't a policy, be honest about what you're thinking. If you make a case that you are looking for time off and are committed to coming back, make sure that you mean that you will indeed come back. If you're not sure you'll come back, then say it and give your company a specific target date when you'll make a decision. It's not fair to have people hold a position open for you for three years while you try to figure out what you're going to do.

Last point on coming back to your job: business and technology change rapidly. In one year, your company can be acquired, use new forms of communication, outsource your entire department, or realize that everyone's skills are obsolete. You may come back to find that your job has been replaced by a chip. While you're away, stay abreast of your industry, company, and team disruptions and changes so you can be prepared for reentry.

Should I Stay or Should I Go?

Dear Someone Else's Dad,
My girlfriend is about to quit her job, and she wants me to do the same so we can buy an RV to explore anywhere we want for a year. She feels she has saved enough, and I guess I have too. The

problem is that I am up for a big promotion in about a year. If I quit now, I'll lose an opportunity that I don't think I'll ever get again. Should I just give it up?

Thanks,

Not So Free-Spirited

Dear NSF-S,

The best I can do is help you set up a framework for your decision without making it sound like an either/or between your girlfriend and your job. The answers to these questions may help you figure out what means the most to you and how much risk you're willing to take. Good luck!

1. The RV adventure. It sounds like a lot of fun. What is the advantage of doing it now versus later? Does the trip need to be for a year? Will you be completely relaxed with your life if you just quit now and go?

2. Your relationship. Will it survive if you don't take the trip at all? If you take another type of trip? If you take the trip as planned?

3. Your job. What's the likelihood of the promotion? What would your work/life be like once you are promoted? Would quitting after you're promoted make sense for your reputation?

4. Quitting now. Do you feel you could get a similar job with a chance of promotion at another firm if you took a year off? Are you committed to starting a brand-new career at a lower level a year from now?

Asking for a Raise or Promotion

Many companies have strict policies on when people can receive raises or promotions. Even still, I've seen people get promoted "off-cycle" because of an immediate vacancy or because of some hush-hush inside machinations. If you feel that you've been passed over for a promotion or raise, you shouldn't let your feelings fester, especially if you think it's about time you moved up or other, less deserving people have bypassed you.

Before we discuss how to make and present an argument about getting a raise, let's talk about why you want a raise versus why you feel you deserve a raise.

Why you want a raise:

- You can't afford to live the life you have with the salary you're making.
- Your friends are making more money than you at their jobs, and you think it's unfair.
- You want to be rich, and you're not getting any younger.
- Money means power, and you want a lot of both.
- Your mom told you that you want a raise.

Why you feel you deserve a raise:

- You haven't had a raise in a long time, and you feel that you should at least get a cost-of-living increase.
- You are ready for more responsibility and a promotion, and both should go along with more money.
- You've made some important gains for the company, and you think that you should be compensated for your share of the success.
- Colleagues at the same level or below are making more money than you, and you think you should be closer to or above parity.
- Your dad told you that you deserve a raise.

All those reasons are very good (sometimes parents are right, after all). But even though you have identified why you deserve a raise, the hard part is asking for one. People face several obstacles:

- They fear they are going to be turned down right away.

- They have a hard time justifying and quantifying their self-worth.

- They are afraid of opening themselves to an emotional conversation, which often happens when people talk about money.

Know Company Policy

As I stated in the section on performance reviews, many companies have strict policies about when employees are eligible for raises and actually tie raises to annual reviews. Still, there's nothing wrong with planting a seed during the year with your managers about getting a raise you feel you deserve.

Even though it may be easier to avoid a face-to-face conversation about money and put all your reasons in emails instead, I recommend doing a combination of both.

Do Research Before Structuring the Message

Assuming you've identified a strong reason why you deserve a raise, Mom notwithstanding, you need to be specific about your reasons, the salary you're looking for, and why it's the appropriate amount. You want to end up with a message that contains two or three bullet points about what you've done to deserve the raise and one bullet point on the salary range you expect based on what you've researched.

The Big Bottom-Line Message

Go back to your reason for wanting a raise and embellish it with a strong statement. You could write something like "I've done amazing work, and I think I should get a raise at the end of the year because I think the company should reward me for my proportionate share of the total upside."

But that would be bad. The sentiment is there, but the message is way too strident and self-absorbed.

Or you could write something like "I hope you might consider giving me a salary bump if you think you can afford it because other people said my work was pretty good. But it's OK if you can't." But that would also be bad. The tone is too apologetic.

Or you could write something like "Over the past year I have been very proud to have worked on many projects, which in part helped the firm reach its revenue targets. Although I recognize that the firm doesn't talk about salary increases until the end of the year, I was hoping you will consider the following when you evaluate my performance."
And that would be great.

The Bullet Points

The list of bullet points is the place to be specific about the work that benefitted the firm in profitability, efficiency, morale, or culture. Name the project, your role, what you did, and the outcome. Feel free to quantify the results if possible. For example:

- "Worked on Rattail project with Nik for three months, compiling data, preparing proposals, responding to client concerns, and launching campaign, which brought in 40 percent more than expected revenue/reduced back-end response time by 20 percent/ brought in greater participation from branch offices, which were very pleased with the outcome (see attached surveys)."

The last bullet point—on how much money you want—is trickiest to get right. If company policy dictates that salary increases will be given in a range of 3 to 8 percent, you may want to say you're hoping to receive a salary increase near the top of the allowed range.

If you feel you're not receiving the appropriate market rate for your work, be sure to research salary ranges for comparable positions in your firm and in local competitors'. Glassdoor, Indeed, Monster, and other sites can help you determine what salaries are reasonable. Caveat: be careful of quoting a salary that is way out of whack with what you're being paid. Your manager could easily say, "Wow, it sounds like our competitors are paying more. Good luck in your new job search to get paid that much. See ya!"

A good third bullet then would be:

- "I am hoping that a salary increase would reflect the work I've done and also be more in line with what other senior associates here at Rankle Corp. and among our competitors are receiving (between X and Y)."

Talk to Your Manager Before Sending the Email

Don't surprise your manager with the email about your salary request. Find a time to mention that you'd like to send your manager a recap of things you are proud to have accomplished over the past year. You can also say that you recognize that your performance review is several months away, but you wanted to document what you've done and mention some issues about salary.

Bonus versus Increase

Companies may keep your base salary constant or even low and give the remainder of compensation in the form of an annual bonus, which at companies like financial services firms is often the largest part of the total package. I would encourage people to prepare the same type of email showing accomplishments to help your managers calculate your bonus. However, if bonuses are tied to performance at your company, I would not recommend quoting an actual figure because you don't know what the entire bonus pool is. Still, you could say something like "I hope you'll consider this information when calculating my bonus this year. As a point of reference, last year my bonus was X."

Hey, I know it's hard for people to ask for more money. In some cultures, it may even be considered rude. But if you feel you deserve a boost, be smart about what you want to say, and ask yourself, "What's the worst thing that could happen?" I think the worst would be that your manager could just say no. If that is indeed the answer, ask for a clear reason, and find out what the future portends. At least you'll be clear on where things stand.

Ghosting or Abandoning Your Job

Dear Someone Else's Dad,

I am a longtime HR generalist and have noticed a trend of young people leaving—I mean leaving suddenly without notifying and not coming back—when they find out they're not getting a promotion. I wish these young people felt they could talk things out with us rather than completely abandoning their companies, many of which are willing to help them succeed. Do you have suggestions to stem this abandonment trend?
Thanks,
HR Lady

Dear HRL,

Ghosting employers is an unfortunate—and inconsiderate—trend. And discussions about performance and promotion have a strong emotional component. In your situation, it sounds like people are jumping ship because they are disappointed, surprised, or embarrassed.

My advice is to be more up front more often with your people about how they are doing. Consider moving from annual reviews to a just-in-time feedback model. Be open with everyone about what's required to earn a promotion. And if you still find that people are disappearing, think about addressing the issue in a town hall meeting to reassure your employees that you want them to flourish in your company and welcome them to talk to you in confidence about any challenges.

How to Quit Gracefully

Change is a part of life. (I love making profound statements like that. Feel free to quote me.) When you decide to leave your job for whatever reason, keep these three words in mind: cash your check. Well, that's not really my advice, but others I know who have left their jobs live by it. My actual three words to keep in mind are: don't burn bridges.

Here's what I mean: though you may be thrilled to leave your job, don't leave on bad terms. In addition, don't bad-mouth your employer or post anything anywhere online about negative experiences. Your professional network is important no matter whether you detest people you used to work with. Here are some advantages of maintaining relationships:

- You may need to ask for references at some point.
- You may find out that they are connected via LinkedIn to people you'd like to meet.
- You may discover that at some point they've also moved on from your old company, which could give you a reason to get back in touch.
- You may find that other people will try to network with you solely because you worked at your previous firm.
- You just never know.

Similar to what I said about investigating policies on sabbaticals, find out the proper protocol for giving notice. If there aren't any formal rules, I suggest you chat first with your supervisor or the person who hired you to explain your decisions and date of departure.

Once your final day has been announced, I also recommend sending an email to everyone on your team—or everyone in your company if you know most people—letting them know how much you've enjoyed your time at the company, thanking them for the experience, and forwarding your new contact information. I'd keep the part about why you're leaving brief; there's no need to say more than one sentence, if anything at all.

I called this section "How to Quit Gracefully" because I wanted to focus on the word *grace*. Many people associate the word with religion, but my association is more related to charm, politeness, and kindness. And why leave a job without having people remember those traits about you?

Is LinkedIn Too Self-Promotional?

Dear Someone Else's Dad,

I'm the only professional woman left on my team since two senior women resigned last month. I'm ready to quit, too, for various reasons, and I want to make a clean break. A friend told me that I should first join LinkedIn and connect with everyone and then quit. Isn't that a bit two-faced and purely opportunistic?
Thanks,
Ready to Leave

Dear RTL,

I see where you're coming from. It's like saying, "Hey, let's be best friends!" on Monday and then saying, "Whoops, sorry, bye, I'll never see you again, have a nice life!" on Thursday. I think you should stay in touch with your current colleagues over LinkedIn, but I'd do it this way: Decide when you're going to leave and resign whenever you're ready. Email everyone to say goodbye and let them know you will be joining LinkedIn shortly and will send them each invitations to connect. This act is not opportunistic, nor is it two-faced. It's just a nice, proper, and professional thing to do. You should also stay in touch with the two (or more) women who left the firm. You never know where those connections can lead.

Fourteen

BE COOL, BE TRUE TO YOURSELF, BE OPEN TO ADVICE

As you've seen throughout this book, people ask me how to deal with situations where they've been treated unfairly. I appreciate the questions, and I'm glad that the people who write didn't automatically think they should have treated the other person unfairly in return. My answers to most questions try to give readers a sense of how to take the high road or be gracious even while working in crappy situations.

I also want to emphasize that no one is in this work thing alone. We all look around and think that everyone else is highly competent and no one else has a whiff of self-doubt. That's just not true. (Honestly, I'd be scared of someone with no self-doubt. That's how autocrats are born.)

Never be afraid to ask someone to explain things to you. Find the people on your team whom you feel will truly want you to succeed. They will love to talk about what they're working on, and even when they spew out too much, you can cull what you need. Just don't forget to paraphrase and ask relevant follow-up questions.

I'm not the arbiter of cool, but I'd consider the person who came to me and asked specific questions (maybe with some small talk peppered in) cooler than people who hide behind screens and try to figure out absolutely everything on their own. Besides, with a conversation I can see their nonverbal communication and discover how the cool person's mind works.

And of course, there's always me, willing to take your questions at dad@someoneelsesdad.com. All emails I published are scrubbed for anonymity in case the writer hasn't done that already. I gladly accept your questions.

I've been very lucky in my career in that I've had a very low percentage of jerky clients. Maybe it's because of self-selection; the jerks feel that they don't need my services. Sure, I've worked with people I might not want to socialize with, but that's OK. As long as we have shared business goals and a sense of respect or grace, I'm happy.

Sometimes, I give people a choice of how they'd like other people to remember them: very diligent, very smart, very resourceful, or very nice. There's no right answer, only the answer that's right for you. But think about the question and think about how you would like the working world to see you. I'm confident you'll make the right choice.

ACKNOWLEDGMENTS

I want to thank all my global clients who have helped me understand first-hand how people think, behave, speak, and write differently around the world. The questions people have asked me about how to communicate effectively, along with my observations, helped me shape what I do for a living and why I enjoy my work so much. I especially thank the young generation of workers who have asked me how to handle their sensitive and embarrassing situations. We learn a lot from each other.

Some of my longtime friends have been extraordinarily generous with their time, expertise, and support in this book's development. Lauren Letellier had some great ideas for some very early chapters. Susan Cohen, a wonderful literary agent, read an early draft, told me how to put a book proposal together, and encouraged me to develop an online presence, so she wouldn't be the only one to laugh at my jokes. Joann Baney, who brought me to the old Professional Development Center at Columbia Business School, has been a great friend and colleague for decades. My former business partners, Brenda Bazan and Shaunna Black, fortuitously said, "Let's call Greenleaf Book Group to see if they like your idea." Chris Fine, one of the most supportive friends anyone could have, contacted me almost daily with encouraging texts and calls. David Farmer has been a champion from the first day I told him about my work and enhanced my digital presence with his terrific creativity. Finally, I'm so fortunate that our dear friends and annual travel companions Kent and Ann Greenawalt allowed me to sit by their lake and write a lot of this book with only occasional interruptions for coffee, laughter, and encouragement.

I received great advice from my "team" of younger professionals, whose support and ideas I truly appreciate: Shadee Tabasi, Eliza Shapiro, John and Becky Boles, Liam and Leslie Kraus, Laura Boles and Seth Brownold, Will Jacobson, Ben Bass, and Jamie Steele.

The team at Greenleaf Book Group has been extraordinary in helping me navigate the dos and don'ts of book publishing. Many thanks to Justin Branch, who so quickly brought me in; Tyler LeBleu, who expertly set up a production schedule, which made me realize we were really going to publish this; Corrin Foster, who made scary social media less scary with her expert advice; Rachael Brandenburg for being a fantastic designer when all I said was that I didn't want to bore people with the cover; Claudia Volkman, Elizabeth Brown, and Jay Hodges, who gave wonderful editorial suggestions and all told me they laughed at least three times. And finally, to my remarkably savvy editor and adviser, Jessica Choi, who was a true partner, virtual handholder, and anxiety reducer throughout the entire process.

Lastly, I am indebted to my adult children, Daniel and Nora Yawitz, who didn't roll their eyes when I told them the title and gave me great advice every day. My parents, Marcia and Burt Yawitz, and my sister, Elizabeth Sehring, have been stalwart supporters through all of my ups and downs, and I thank them for believing in me. Most importantly, I want to thank my wife, Carol Phethean, who for over 36 years has given me truly the best guidance, which has taken me to places that I never dreamed of going.

INDEX